Managing Technology in Our Schools

Establishing Goals and Creating a Plan

Betsy Price

ROWMAN & LITTLEFIELD EDUCATION
Lanham • New York • Toronto • Plymouth, UK

Published in the United States of America
by Rowman & Littlefield Education
A Division of Rowman & Littlefield Publishers, Inc.
A wholly owned subsidiary of The Rowman & Littlefield Publishing Group, Inc.
4501 Forbes Boulevard, Suite 200, Lanham, Maryland 20706
www.rowmaneducation.com

Estover Road
Plymouth PL6 7PY
United Kingdom

British Library Cataloguing in Publication Information Available

Library of Congress Cataloging-in-Publication Data

Price, Betsy, 1949–
    Managing technology in our schools : establishing goals and creating a plan / Betsy
Price.
        p. cm.
    ISBN-13: 978-1-57886-677-9 (cloth : alk. paper)
    ISBN-10: 1-57886-677-4 (cloth : alk. paper)
    ISBN-13: 978-1-57886-678-6 (pbk. : alk. paper)
    ISBN-10: 1-57886-678-2 (pbk. : alk. paper)
  1. Educational technology—Planning. 2. School management and organization. I. Title.
    LB1028.3.P76 2007
    371.33—dc22
                                                          2007027912

Contents

Acknowledgements

This book talks about the energy of the teachers and administrators who are early adopters of technology in schools and how it is a paramount trait to successful technology integration. However, the energy of innovators and monetary risk takers outside the school community also needs to be infused to lend their expertise in business and public relations. These people bet their talents and money to build the products and tools schools need. I also want to thank the mentors and role models I had, Dorothy Dart and Robin Heyden, who are not only good examples of women of vision but business persons who also set goals and accomplish what they set out to do. I also want to thank Scott Taylor for his loyalty to people and ideas.

I have had the good fortune to work with many talented and innovative educators and scientists in the school systems who have, through their dedication to students, provided me with solid examples of all that is good in our schools. Every one of these people shared their world with me without hesitation, candidly and honestly. They are the backbone of this book.

You open a book and for some unknown reason you read the acknowledgements. Yada Yada Yada. The author always finds a literary way to apologize to family and friends for menopausal-like behavior during the time writing the book. Now, after writing one, I understand why they gush these statements out. I also want to guiltily and humbly thank the people I love who are amazingly still hanging with me after a year and a half of menopausal-like behavior.

Chapter One

Technology Meanders In

Success in managing technology and technology budgets in schools rests less on business managers' expertise in accounting, pedagogy, or technology than on their expertise and skill in mediation. The expectation has been (crossed fingers) that technology would reveal the elusive silver bullet—that one perfect classroom program that works for every student and is easy on the budget, easy to finance, and easy to administer. This has not happened because technology has not yet been in the classroom in any big way. Schools first wired rooms according to what they could afford; hence, technology first landed in the central office, then the library, and then shared labs. As each area plugged in, it beefed up what they did. Support services that were once auxiliary became strong partners for teaching. The result was that in order to get technology integrated into the curriculum, business managers found themselves managing more people and more equipment and blending more skills than predicted. This roundabout way of getting it there puts technology at the tipping point to fill its big promises for learning. The magic bullet will be local solutions for local problems.

Now that computers are entering the classrooms, teachers are plugging in and saying, "And . . . ?" The electronic curriculum they expected is not there. But that is okay. Teachers expect more than what was first offered. Teachers now want technology to be a tool for teaching that gives them control to choose the right programs for their students in their class on a particular day. They are no longer looking for the one learning program that fits all students. This is made possible by the enriched data coming from the central office, which produces more diagnostic tools to analyze just what learning solution students need. Teachers also have enriched electronic services provided by the library, which supplies more opportunities for students to build information management skills and practice applying them to real-life problems presented in the classroom. Early adopters have experimented with every classroom design and configuration, so they better understand that technology will work in ways other than plugging each kid into a computer.

The more effective role of support services in helping to build electronic curriculum and learning-targeted programs is creating a new paradigm of thinking: local solutions for local problems. Because of the rich array of ways in which technology can deliver curriculum and the ways in which students can choose to access it in or out of school, teachers can easily pick and choose electronic materials that fit the needs of their students when the needs occur. Teachers within one school can select specific activities for targeted learning challenges for just one student, a specific developmental group, or a classroom at a time. In addition, the results from accountability measures like program evaluations and reports to funders let educators know about what others have accomplished and what works.

Other models for electronic curriculum have emerged from an interesting source: the research exhibit designers and museum educators have conducted and use to build exhibits. They have perfected how to use novelty, interaction, and common language to engage, motivate, and guide visitors to learn in a stimulating, charged atmosphere. This knowledge can be directly applied to building electronic materials, which can be a powerful combination of learning from a museum exhibit and from a textbook.

Creating a technology-rich learning environment is no longer just a matter-of-fact, automatic process set in motion by past years of experience and routine. It is the coordination of a complex infrastructure of technology, computers, printers, auxiliary equipment, networks, operating systems, upgrades, maintenance, and repair. It is the creation of atmospheres for learning with the right mix of technology for the subject or task at hand. All of this has to be adapted to the confines of old school buildings, which have limited flexibility for accommodating technology that needs more electrical outlets and Internet connections, larger work tables, more space for the teacher's equipment, more room for students to move around, and more places to hide cables that link computers and auxiliary equipment. Creating a technology-rich learning environment also means working with technical staff members who come from industry and have different expectations and ways of accomplishing tasks. They do not always come from or understand the culture of educators.

The biggest change is that business managers are asking questions differently. It took a long time to build an infrastructure in a fragile time when innovation and experimentation flew by. Educators were asking how they could get technology and what kind was needed. They looked to technology staff and sellers to provide the answers. Now, infrastructures are more stable and teachers are more experienced and knowledgeable, so the question is reversed. Educators are deciding want they want to do pedagogically and charging the technology people to find a way in which they can do it. Business managers have to mediate the process.

All of this happened because of the differences in the ways in which business and schools started to use technology. Businesses bought computers after software was developed; schools took an opposite track and adopted hardware first. They did not have a clear model of how they were going to use it, nor did they know how they were going to finance it, but they knew they had to have it. The cold shower happened when schools discovered that budgets had to be refigured, teachers had to change how they taught, facilities had to be altered, central office staff had to become data miners, and professional technical support staff had to be recruited and hired. This complete disruption of everything and cajoling everyone to play together nicely showed that technology governance and management are the two keys to success. This next step requires business managers to be mediators and arbitrators as well as managers and overseers of budgets—budgets that also became more complicated.

The organizational challenge for business managers lies in the unique ruling regime of schools, a feudal system with stacks of stakeholders: parents, local and national businesses, teachers, principals, professional organizations, district administrators, state legislators, state boards of education, the federal government, and so on. Money, policies, procedures, and goals for technology come from all of these sources and, more often than not, arrive out of concert with each other. The stakeholders all have different reasons for why, how, and when they want to bring technology into schools. They also have some interesting and creative ways in which to fund their initiatives. The result of this is that money and attention are not always distributed evenly among schools or even tempered in any way; hence, they often come as torrential rainfalls to some schools while others experience parching drought conditions. This is not going to change, but it can be managed cleverly to give local schools local control.

In the past, the unpredictable funding and kings and queens at every white tower caused schools to sometimes take small steps and other times take unprecedented whopping leaps toward adopting technology. This game of Mother May I? resulted in fragmented technology integration. A school would get one hundred thousand dollars for doing this or a mandate but no money to do that. And, to make it more interesting, schools often had a choice in whether or not to proceed, even if it meant dragging their feet. Each school was left on its own to decide when to play and when not to play. Playing meant being aggressive in treasure hunting and, when the treasure was found, setting up a unique technology infrastructure. Schools acted independently with funds from various sources to push forward at their own speeds. The advantage of all this was that it gave schools the unanticipated opportunity to experiment on a small, affordable scale with electronic delivery of the curriculum and with the employment of learning tools without making a large expensive purchase.

There is another reason besides finances and too many feudal layers that kept total adoption at bay. Paradoxically, technology held itself back. In the face of an alarming rate of change and innovation, schools' fear and self-preservation kept educational technology anchored to the past and anxious about the future. There were always new computers, new software, and new updates. The insecurities surrounding what to buy and when to buy caused schools not to buy. It was a catch-22. Schools had to be made to purchase a technology wild with innovation and change. However, they would also have to be crazy to have no interest in something with such dynamic potential for improving teaching and learning.

During the dot-com boom, the model that everyone envisioned of a technology-rich classroom was that of happy schoolchildren, each with his or her very own computer, learning away by surfing the Internet to discover and gain new knowledge. It was a grand vision, but there were over sixty million students in public schools from kindergarten through high school. This meant that schools would have had to purchase sixty million computers and another four million for teachers. But if every school in the country had succumbed to the hype and mortgaged the buildings to purchase computers and Internet connections, the advancement of educational technology would have come to a complete, 100 percent, screeching halt. They would have been stuck with obsolete computers, software, and operating systems to the tune of millions of dollars.

Thankfully, schools did not bankrupt themselves with this initial massive expenditure. But they were clearly big future customers, and this kept hope burning for the technology companies' CEOs, salespersons, and stockholders, who were anticipating the time when schools would purchase en masse millions of computers, one for each student's desk. Not being financially able to do that, schools only purchased enough computers to keep the investors investing at a steady pace. This was the carrot that kept venture capitalists throwing money at developers, but the dot-com bubble burst and some analysts determined that it was because there were not enough managers and business experts to evaluate the markets and control the pace of development. At the same time, other analysts said that such unbridled behavior was needed to fuel innovation. True, it was probably a blessing that the computer geeks and venture capitalists continued working, poking at the glasses sliding down their noses with nary a worry about money.

The lack of planning was a good thing for schools also. If anyone had calculated how long it would take to create a technological infrastructure in schools, the movement would have died. Dead. Never breathed a breath. Imagine telling educators in 1993, who were contemplating a mere four-thousand-dollar computer purchase, that this one computer would eventually avalanche to an unstoppable, oozing landslide of budget changes and that almost one-third of the school's and the district's money would be diverted to technology-related expenses. Each school would add new technical staff positions instead of teachers, and districts would need to add even more. All this would come out of an ever-shrinking educational financial pie. It was not a good base from which to launch a learning revolution.

Getting computers into the classroom was not an easy task. Over sixty-one thousand public schools needed to be wired from top to bottom. If all of these schools were new, it would have been a small challenge, but most of them were old, with unyielding and unforgiving stone, plaster, and asbestos walls. Each old school had to run a tangled web of wires through miles of hanging tubes taped or nailed to walls, lower ceilings to hide and protect the cables, or raise floors to prevent students from tripping over proliferating wires and cords.

So before any grand dynamic revolution could happen, schools had to find the money to finance everything. Imagine going into a potential funding agency or local bank to ask them for hundreds of millions of dollars to purchase something that only a few people knew about, having no clear idea as to how it was going to be used, but knowing it was going to be really, really, really great. Schools actually did this successfully and amazingly raised money on nothing more than a vision, a handful of dreams. The early principals, superintendents, and school boards were pretty remarkable people to have received a penny; they were part grand visionaries and part snake-oil salesmen.

Much of the speech making used to gain technology money included the proclamation that once the infrastructure was complete, the Internet would be chock-full of wonderful and free-of-charge content written by scientists and other academics in their spare time. As soon as schools lined up computers in neat rows and paired each one up with a student, learning would begin. But things didn't happen quite the way early developers expected. What it did do, lucky for them, was dispel some of the myths surrounding educational technology.

The first myth dispelled was that schools would ever be able to afford, or even need, one working computer per student. This book supports the premise that individual computers are not necessarily required or, in fact, really that important in creating a technology-rich classroom and ongoing learning environment. The integration of various types of technology and programs into traditional teaching can increase and enhance interactions among teachers, students, and parents. New cognitive science research has proven that students learn differently. Not all students will learn through interactive electronic activities, and not all students will learn by reading a textbook. Lessons from the informal education community on how they use exhibits that have captured the essence and spirit of social interaction and learning can be applied to organizing students to optimally and appropriately use technology.

The second myth was that the Internet would supply an overabundance of free-of-charge volunteer-produced curricula. Scientists, historians, and behavioral scientists are not going to be able to write content and lesson plans and post them on the Internet in their spare time. Content is not going to be free. In fact, the Internet has become a graveyard of free projects that, without sustainable funds or personalities, are unfinished and abandoned. That being said, the Internet is chock-full of brilliantly and professionally produced materials. But for teachers to use them, they need a better system for finding these sites than devoting an entire Sunday afternoon to searching, filtering, and rewriting.

The third myth was that teachers would be the sole key players in using computers to support learning. That myth was completely dispelled when computers enlightened and empowered staff in areas of schools that are not teacher directed and controlled: the central office for data collection and the library for information management. Technology is the tool that amplifies the ability for teachers to have diagnostic data that is efficiently collected, flexible, and easy to analyze so that it can have more impact on diagnostic teaching. College-bound and career-bound students must prioritize library and information management skills so they can be prepared for jobs at the local plumbing supply store or as the next president of the United States.

The real time for integrating technology into the curriculum is today. The next step is to develop the electronic curriculum: an entire year of lessons and activities that teachers and students have access to when they need them, as they need them, and learning-targeted programs to address special challenges. The reason this had not developed before is that for the last thirteen years schools have been devoted to building a physical infrastructure. To the credit of PVC pipe, home improvement stores, innovative thinkers, and risk takers, schools moved forward despite old, impermeable walls, floors, and ceilings to build a technological infrastructure. The foundation is strong, and the infrastructure is mature. Accomplishing this was a very, very big project.

Developing and selling curricula will start a new boom in the commercial sector, igniting the same gold-rush spirit that the dot-com era generated as new and less-encumbered smaller businesses smell the profit in a sound product and respond. The forerunners will be those that match local learning challenges with local learning solutions that support diverse learning styles, abilities, and preferences, create an effective twenty-four-hour, seven-days-per-week environment, and make technology flexible enough to fit the physical constraints of school buildings. For those businesses that are right now raising their hands bouncing up and down exclaiming, "We have it! We have it!" there needs to be a better system for connecting smaller companies to schools. The massive sales machine of the large publishing companies can be a roadblock to teachers finding new can-turn-on-a-dime companies and new companies finding teachers who need solutions.

Throughout this book it will be suggested how, where, and when business managers need to mediate among stakeholders. This is not going to be easy because it is an environment that is used to being run by independent operators. Mediation means that business managers have to help teachers and staff to identify what they want to achieve and establish realistic goals for success. The word *mediate* is used rather than *negotiate*, *cajole*, or *manage* because people are going to argue and fuss as roles evolve and the business manager will spend a lot of time refereeing. Hence the term *mediate* is used rather than *manage* or *pull by the ear*. Business managers and teachers need to work with technical staff and software designers to figure out how electronic materials will be built within the school's boundaries of facilities, money, and expertise.

Schools are now at a tipping point for change, about to incorporate technology as never before in the final frontier, the classroom. For this to happen, the input of savvy business managers is required. This book is for those who will not only be responsible for managing and financing technology budgets but for providing the leadership to govern. The book reflects on the last thirteen years of schools' roundabout progress and uses the lessons learned to identify best practices for managing and financing the next wave of technology purchases and applications. It will highlight the perseverance and persistence that adopting technology required from the beginning and what is needed today as technology matures from a hyped-up dream into an established, solid support and tool for teaching. The purpose is by no means to expose the frailties or berate the progress of the system; that has already been done many times by many authors. It is no longer fun to read or to write about it. The goals are to identify and highlight for business managers what works well and how that knowledge can be applied to improving the management of this important contribution to learning.

To do this, this book will explore the political, economic, physical, and staff realities of schools, which business management must address in order to continue the process of educating the next generation of technologically savvy, intellectual, problem-solving workers. The thoughts in this book are from the perspective of an observer watching schools and teachers as they pioneer electronic curricula. Case studies will be given to illustrate how technology was brought in, who paid, and how it was managed. These observations show the complexity and the need for forward-thinking management that can mediate among stakeholders, fostering technology as a tool, not the mythical silver bullet. They also show that the next large purchases in technology will be electronic curricul that deliver a wide variety of materials employing different teaching techniques.

But before the commercial folks start counting their profits and schools see improved teaching and learning, everyone will see that the rules about how schools purchase curricula have changed. Parents, legislators, educators, and administrators, wiser about the goals, potential, and realities of using technology to teach, will require that companies give documentation that their products work based on quantitative and qualitative evaluative measurements. Technology is no longer a fluffy novelty that supplements the curriculum to entertain students. The age of accountability is upon us. The rigor and quality of an electronic curriculum will have to be high.

This book will look at why the age of educational technology begins tomorrow and why governance has to be integrated into all areas of schools for effective management. The key is that technology provides local solutions to local problems. As Dr. Laura says, this is my advice; you may take it, leave it, or adopt it into your own practices.

Chapter Two

The First Buyers
Early Adopters of Technology

To manage technology, it is important to understand who brought technology into the schools, from where the money came, and what factors influenced its purchase. In the early days, there was no business model that showed who would purchase technology, how it would be funded, and where it would be used. As a result, there were many stakeholders, all of whom had some control over school finances, working hard to bring in the type of technology that they believed useful. This chapter discusses one of these groups of stakeholders: the early adopters, a small but powerful group of teachers who were the first to bring in technology. They organized a chaotic system of haphazard adoption, provided consistency for training and tech support, and plowed through the difficulties to achieve an infrastructure. They started the important process of identifying how technology would enrich teaching and learning. They were divining rods that discovered outside sources for funding, but they also created havoc.

Early adopters began to appear in large numbers during the dot-com era, when the literature and popular press were chock-full of articles about the wonders of using technology for teaching, as if changing teaching styles was as easy as breathing. The hype far exceeded the reality. Like many trends in education, the use of the Internet was well publicized without actually happening in any big way in the schools. However, influences from the media and press played an important role in keeping the dream alive as early adopters braved the too-often hostile environment for non–tech savvy teachers and gradually made the hype real.

In the beginning, the Internet was not user-friendly; in fact, it was just plain painful. Using the Internet meant learning a new language that was evolving daily and had no dictionary. Software was named after people's dogs, favorite animals, or comic book characters. In order to use FTP (File-Transfer Protocol), you had to know how to use Gopher or, later, Archie, or, if you were a Mac owner, you could use Fetch. There were no pretty pictures to ease the way, just acres and acres of text and symbols.

The teacher-hostile environment emerged because the first large body of users and developers were scientists. They were not necessarily an unfriendly bunch, but they were primarily focused on science and had little time to consider that the Internet needed to be visually pleasing if its use was to become widespread. Luckily, nestled in the midst of the scientists were groups of far-sighted graduate students and professors who were interested in making the Internet user-friendly to a broader audience. One group, at the University of Illinois, developed Mosaic, the forerunner of the commercial browsers like Netscape and Explorer. Mosaic was a piece of software that collected individual files from one computer and arranged them in an attractive array of pictures and text on another computer.

Mosaic displayed material in a way that was more conscious of what pop culture would find attractive. This was an important factor in changing the lackluster pace at which schools acquired technology. Until then, computers and the Internet had made only a small impact on schools or individual users. Mosaic changed that. It brought pictures, music, animation, and color to computers, all with just one click. The Internet had been around since the 1980s, but this pizzazz and sparkle catapulted it into the public eye, making it the absolute, must-have rage.

Although prettying up the Internet made it hot to have, it didn't change the fact that schools were still struggling with how to get the infrastructure they needed to manage hundreds of computers. Early adopters, teachers who were not willing to wait for schools to get connected or provide them with reliable 24/7 service, connected themselves by going through private Internet providers. This was done at great personal expense, paying per minute for use. These early adopters learned HTML (Hyper-Text Markup Language), the language of the Internet; figured out how to set up computers; and logged on to every site funded by NSF (National Science Foundation), other government agencies, and private foundations. They had to learn how to troubleshoot software, download new updates, and, dangerously armed with screwdrivers, even fix their computers. They hooked up microscopes, Palm Pilots, printers, probes, wind tunnels, and televisions. Nothing was safe. When they were done doing all that, they ran around and recruited other teachers to technology. They were busy, busy people.

Mosaic was wonderful, but it also made the computers and auxiliary equipment that teachers were using obsolete. This was the beginning of the industry's disruptive pattern. With each new innovation that made the Internet a more useful tool, schools had to scurry to upgrade, update, and buy more of whatever. The changes also left teachers, who had made a commitment of time and effort to get trained and proficient, suddenly having to play by a new set of rules. This churning innovation created a market for new and better projects, but also made many administrators and teachers cautious about purchasing technology. Innovation was happening so quickly that a large purchase would have left schools owning obsolete equipment within a year or two. Schools faced a dilemma: At what point in time could computers be purchased en masse without becoming obsolete by the time they were set up? A common proclamation by teachers and administrators was, "We'll buy when computer technology stabilizes."

But early adopters found ways to acquire new technology or upgrade the old. They contributed by keeping technology in the schools when large purchases seemed too risky. While the entire school could not afford to keep up, the early adopters could. Lone buyers, and only a handful in the schools, were able to make small but influential purchases, keeping technology alive and giving heart to developers. They brought technology in, used it, and passed it down to other teachers as they constantly upgraded to the latest bright and shiny teaching tool. They discovered that other teachers were happy to inherit and use the computers until they slowly and painfully died under the barrage of student use.

Much of their funding came from the National Science Foundation (NSF). Early on, NSF "owned" the Internet, which was not accessible to the public. However, NSF administrators realized that they could not continue funding the Internet forever. There had to be some way to make it pay for itself. Technology needed financing, and that meant creating demand from a large market. The nation's four million teachers and sixty million students were just that. Companies adopted the NSF model, offered everything for free, and then began to lure early adopters with workshops, technology they could take home, and prestige. But attracting new users to a not-so-friendly Internet was the challenge. Their solution was to provide seed money to educators to attract them. The early adopters eagerly stepped forth. Workshops were created to train teachers in how to use the Internet and the funded sites. When NSF opened up to industry, they too discovered the power of early adopters, and they invested in them by offering advanced workshops and training on how to use their products and services.

An example is Genentech, a pioneering biotechnology company that wanted to quickly create a pipeline of teachers to help produce the large numbers of biotech workers that are required by a booming industry. Genentech partnered with the National Science Teachers Association (NSTA) to create an Internet program that would reach teachers nationally. They launched Access Excellence, an Internet forum and idea exchange exclusively for science teachers. Teachers could share their favorite classroom activities, have access to scientists, and network with each other. Genentech created a fellows program where early adopters, in exchange for a plane ticket to California and a free computer, helped the company to develop and promote the program. Each year more fellows were recruited to review the previous year's progress and to add new materials. They gave presentations to professional organizations, wrote articles, generated excitement, and publicized the Genentech name.

Another private company benefited by participating in teachers' community activities. Not all applicants got to be fellows, but anyone who applied was given a free AOL (America Online) account to access the Internet and free hours. The success of the project benefited AOL because they gained thousands of new and loyal members who eventually became paying customers when their special offers ran out. Although it does not seem significant now, teachers were given unlimited, free hours of Internet service, and that was a welcome relief from what they were paying. The free resources were magic. Teachers loved AOL.

Many other companies joined in to bring teachers to their sites. A lesson plan for the first through third grades would attract hundreds of thousands of teachers to a site. They also offered training, grants, and free materials. Of course, the activities usually required that the teachers use their products. The business community relied on early adopters to attract other teachers to these sites, gain potential buyers, and win community goodwill. Schools relied on early adopters to share these resources with other teachers, to entice peers to go online, and to enrich teaching.

Early adopters proved to be effective sellers of technology to their peers. Expertly trained and armed with free computers from these projects, they were a constant presence in the schools. They were like those annoying people who quit smoking, find religion, or read *Consumers Reports*. They made a tremendous contribution by being there, being consistent, and continually adapting as the Internet and technology changed. They held workshops wherever they found a venue, even informally as they walked down the halls. Although other teachers lived in fear of technology, they soon caved in and followed the pied pipers.

Another contribution of early adopters was the discovery of an unanticipated benefit to using the Internet: online discussion groups that formed national communities. It was an important contribution. Teachers interact with students most of the day. They don't have much of an opportunity to network with peers because classrooms walls create a physical separation. During the times that they don't teach, they have other responsibilities that inhibit socializing, such as hall monitoring, grading, and scholarly duties like curriculum development. The Internet addressed this problem of isolation by bringing communities of like-minded teachers together through listservs (online discussion groups).

With listservs, teachers could choose when to participate. They could respond at their own convenience, not when the phone rang or when a workshop was scheduled. A teacher in New York could send a message to her community pal in San Francisco who was still sleeping or to the teacher down the hall who always raced home to take care of his children. Maintaining communication before and after professional-development activities was also important. Conversations, collaborations, and relationships with peers cultivated at professional conferences could now continue long after everyone was back at school.

Computer companies, developers of electronic equipment, and makers of auxiliary equipment recognized that these listersvs were a powerful way to get out their information. Early adopters would spend hours surfing the new Web sites, evaluating them for quality, and then broadcasting to other teachers which sites were the best. The same was true for computer and auxiliary equipment. A good word on a listserv was sure to sell a product. Companies could not buy that type of advertising, and they rewarded teachers well to gain that endorsement.

It is important for managers to understand the power of early adopters. Early adopters kept a candle burning in the schoolhouse window for industry and for schools. They made important contributions to bringing technology to schools in a way that provided stability and solidity. They attracted grant money, free equipment, and leadership. The academic freedom that allows teachers to act independently enabled this. Had they been forced to march with the majority and wait until this Internet thing caught on, technology wouldn't have been put into the schools until today. Their power remains today, and they will carry schools through the next innovation. They are an important group to cultivate.

However, not all that occurred was positive. The process was messy and sometimes ugly. Early adopters running amok often broadsided administrators by obtaining only half of the computers that they really needed and collecting equipment brands that were not compatible or auxiliary equipment without the computer. They needed the school to provide the rest of the money and support. In schools without financial and managerial infrastructure, early adopters' contributions often caused schools to have to abruptly find unbudgeted money to supplement what grants did not pay for, add additional staff time, and sometimes absorb failed projects. Early adopters also created a climate of teachers who have computers and those who do not, and, left unchecked by management, this created animosity among teachers. It resulted in some students having a technology-rich curriculum while other did not. Not content with alienating their fellow teachers, early adopters completely annoyed technical staff, who had a hard time keeping up with urgent demands. As they lead the adoption of the next innovation, this is unlikely to change.

SUMMARY

Early adopters were pivotal to the adoption of computers and the Internet and are key to any innovation in schools. They are risk takers, trendsetters, and evangelists of any movement. Teachers who bounded ahead of the comfort level of the school to finance the innovation and then to maintain it were not always a pleasant experience for administrators. Because technology disrupted regular classroom and school routine, early adopters often irritated other teachers, who were desperately trying to ensure that routine reigned supreme. They also continually clashed with the very persons they had made it a necessity to hire, the systems managers and technology staff. To continue with innovations, business managers need to understand the importance of early adopters but also formulate methods to channel and guide their energy and boldness.

Chapter Three

Managing Innovation

In the early stages of schools building technology infrastructure, it was interesting to watch administrators react to early adopters. It was very apparent that teachers who used technology got technology from wherever. There was not enough technology sprinkling down from stakeholders to support every room in the school; however, it was sufficient, even generous, for a couple of classrooms. The extra money and equipment that early adopters bought in was essential for progress. Administrators were under pressure to get the computers to the students, and the easiest way to do this was to reward early adopters, who were interested in using technology and had a plan of how it might be used. To seed technological innovation, wise managers crossed their fingers, closed their eyes, and encouraged, even nurtured, the chaos in order to capture early adopters' undocumented money and speed the progress of bringing technology into the school. Cultivating and protecting early adopters for the benefit of the entire school is always valid; however, business managers have to factor their care and feeding into the bigger picture of technology, not just the world of a single classroom.

All of this requires that business managers recognize early adopters' value in spreading innovation to the second wave of teachers and devise ways in which to encourage early adopters to pursue their exploration of new stuff and funds while keeping innovation manageable. Business managers can do this by cultivating interaction and communication among teachers and staff, bringing them together for regular discussion, debate, and strategic planning on how technology should be governed. This includes providing early adopters with the freedom, safety, and resources to explore; establishing a way for them to exchange information with other teachers and staff; and budgeting for their successes as well as their occasional blunders.

ENCOURAGE PROFESSIONAL ORGANIZATIONS

Encourage early adopters to be active in national, regional, and local professional development organizations. Besides the obvious benefits to teacher's personal scholarly development and enrichment, professional organizations are the best way for them to network with national peers, higher-educational institutions, government funders, and companies. These are all sources of grants, workshops, and other opportunities to feed their addiction to the new and cool at bargain-basement costs or often for free. Because of the Internet, teachers keep active in professional organizations long after the national conferences are over through listservs, Web sites, and e-mail correspondence. The important networking they do builds relationships with other early adopters.

Professional organizations are the best way for companies to connect to the strong and powerful core of teachers who will become the evangelists of their product. Convention exhibitors will court, entice, and lure teachers to their booths with t-shirts, bouncing balls, free products, dinners, entertainment, and conversation. But they also give out free workshops, equipment, materials, lesson plans, and anything else that they can use to educate teachers about their products. An example is the National Education Computing Conference (NECC), the annual event for the International Institute for Technology in Education. Every year it hosts thousands of teachers. It is the largest education-technology exhibit in the world with over four hundred exhibitors, all with high hopes that conference attendees will return to their schools and districts and spread the word. When managers wonder when early adopters do their planning and what they will be purchasing the next year, they need wonder no more. They can see their future in the list of exhibitors and the topics of the scholarly sessions at NECC.

ENCOURAGE EARLY ADOPTERS
TO PURSUE ALTERNATIVE FUNDING

There are many ways to finance professional development and to send early adopters to conferences besides cash out of the school budget. Professional organizations offer scholarships, reduced prices for presenters, or supplemental money to first-time visitors. Volunteer officers often receive free travel, and invited speakers receive funding. Companies give money to teachers for presenting their products at their booth or for a scholarly presentation. Money can also be found through earmarked professional development funds from state and federal sources, many of which are not always used. Grants usually include money for travel to conferences for dissemination of information about how the grant was administered, the outcome measures, and the results of the evaluation.

Most professional opportunities are advertised on the Internet, but it takes some doing to find them all. Early adopters will spend hours looking and will also receive notices through e-mail and other electronic means from the people in their networks. Once the opportunities are found, the intranet is also an important way for early adopters to trigger the e-mail flow of information, news, and tips to other teachers in the school. Attendees of workshops and conferences often report that they received the information secondhand from someone who forwarded an e-mail, tackled them in the halls, or downloaded a PDF (Portable Document Format) file from the Internet and printed and posted it in the teachers lounge. Business managers need to establish ways to reward those who keep networking and searching for information and provide ways for prospecting teachers to share.

There is a negative trade-off when teachers win a trip to a three- or four-day conference or workshop. Conferences are often during the school year, and if the teacher is an officer of an organization, he or she may be required to attend board meetings, arrive before the conference for planning, or attend wrap-up meetings afterward. Teachers need the time off to attend conferences, and that means hiring a substitute and doing some careful lesson planning. It is disruptive to students if substitutes are not used effectively and there is a break in routine. Technology can be of great assistance here. While teachers are at a conference, classroom management software connects them to their classes. A hybrid format combines features of distance education delivered electronically with face-to-face classes while teachers are at the school. Teachers can administer tests electronically on a day when they are gone, have the students do online activities, or give the substitute a step-by-step lesson plan complete with PowerPoint, demonstrations, and activities. The teacher can also be there virtually by prerecording a video cast of a lecture, doing a live video cast, or conducting online chats.

One demographic of teachers who cannot always take advantage of out-of-town opportunities are teachers in mid-career. Often, these teachers have survived their first five years of teaching and will be there for another twenty years, and they need to be included in professional development. Most of the teachers who attend national conferences or workshops are younger, have not started their families, are new to teaching, or are empty nesters and close to retirement. Even if a teacher can find money to go to a conference, teachers with children are often financially handicapped by the additional cost and family obligations of leaving the family behind or taking them along. Not all teachers can attend conferences because using vacation, winter holidays, national holidays, spring break, or summer to travel to workshops and conferences is a luxury.

Technology comes to the rescue when teachers cannot attend in person. There are many ways in which teachers can attend conferences and workshops through electronic communications. Webinars, closed-circuit television, and teleconferencing are ways in which seminars are conducted remotely via the Internet. They allow two-way communication so that participants can be interactive, listen to a presentation or panel, and then participate in the follow-up discussion. A professional or trained moderator facilitates the session using lecture, discussion, and even interactive activities. As at a conference, the participants meet together with those with like interests so they can start networking.

ENCOURAGE BETA TESTING OF NEW PRODUCTS

Business managers should encourage teachers to beta test new products as they come out. In the 1990s, commercial software companies, eager to get their innovative and new products to market, found that the best way was to give them away free to early adopters. In exchange for this, companies were able to get their products beta tested by thousands of teachers, who helped guide the development of the products. This was a cost-winning trade-off for them. New software and hardware are very fragile; bugs appear everywhere. It would cost millions of dollars and almost as many hours to hire a team of people to crawl through a new program and find all that needs to be fixed.

Early adopters began with the 1.01 edition of a product and tested it through 1.02, 1.03, 1.04, and so on. With each new edition, the software strengthened and bugs were worked out. When the schools were ready to spend money, the product was teacher tested and tried and true—well, not always, but reasonably stable. Many technology programs are developed by people without extensive classroom experience, so when programs are put in front of students on a regular day, they prove to be unsuitable for the realities of what can and can't be done. Through beta testing, schools are able to try out technology with a small investment and with small impact if it doesn't work. That is the magic of pilot testing and the benefit for schools. Early adopters are willing to take pains for their cause, and this paves the way for the next round of adopters, who demand a simple, stable, working tool.

Not all companies really and truly want their product to be beta-tested or pilot tested. Some are anticipating selling their product. That is perfectly fine, as long as the business manager, teachers, and staff believe that the product is in line with what might be purchased and that the test will help in the decision. If the product is an innovative and edgy product that an energetic early adopter bumped into, then there needs to be serious discussion and consideration to ensure that there is no obligation for the school to purchase the product and that the time the early adopter devotes to the product is within the teaching goals of the school. Business managers need to be sure that the beta test does not require purchasing expensive auxiliary equipment that will be useless without the program. There are two ways to make sure that this is a legitimate beta test. One is to ask for a signed agreement about the details of the test. The other is to be sure that there is a valid evaluation and that, good, bad, or ugly, the information will be disseminated through scholarly or teacher-practitioner journals.

Business managers need to make it clear that early adopters need to communicate before they commit the school to any beta testing that may require a cash, facility, or in-kind investment. This requires sensitivity, because it is important to stretch the vision of the school and encourage early adopters to reach out for innovation as long as they and the business manager understand that there are no free kittens. Business managers cannot have thirty widgets that won't plug into the whatzits. They can prevent this by mediating between technology staff and teachers as they think through each project. The question is always how can we do this, not why can't we do this.

PROVIDE EARLY ADOPTERS WITH SUPPORT

True giveaways of equipment, programs, and professional development activities will be highly competitive, and many teachers will apply. The sponsors understand that early adopters will be anxious to try anything but that without support from the school the test may not happen, or worse, go badly. They have to be selective, and teachers who have support from the school will be put on the top of the list. Grant funders and companies that come bearing gifts to early adopters will require a letter of support from the administration to be sure that the early adopters have permission and support from the administration to accomplish what they have agreed to do. These letters carry a lot of weight and are often viewed before any of the applicant information is considered. This letter is usually the first impression funders will have of the school and should reflect the professionalism of the administration and the teachers. Of course, the grammar, composition, and spelling of any supportive application or letter should reflect the academic and management level of the school.

Before writing a letter of support, business managers should read the specifications of the grant or offer and ensure that the teacher background, appropriate facilities, and computer support meet the qualifications. The letter should explain why that teacher is uniquely qualified to perform the task or project. It should also explain why the school would be the best choice to do the project. If the application requires a commitment from the school to sustain the project, buy auxiliary equipment, provide space, or make a financial contribution, it should be clearly stated that the school accepts its responsibilities and will support the teacher and the project to the best of its ability. This may even require a letter from the technical staff on how they will accommodate and support any equipment or program.

ENCOURAGE EVALUATION AND ASSESSMENT OF PRODUCTS AND TEACHING METHODS

Early adopters have the opportunity to evaluate and assess programs before schools make large purchases. They are science laboratories for investigating the effectiveness of student learning. It is already understood that one simple program is not going to be the silver bullet that schools were searching for; however, it is going to be that tool that will help students by using them in the class and out. Early adopters need to be more than just the first teachers to use a program—they also need to do the evaluation to answer exactly what the program can and cannot do for students. Does it present the materials that help C students rise to a B level in math? Does it help students whose second language is English excel in writing? Does it help teachers to grade essay questions so they can provide more feedback and constant feedback to students? Are the results applicable to a learning challenge, grade level, or discipline on a regional or national level?

Evaluation of educational programs can be a very complicated and often messy process, but it is worth the time and effort for early adopters to keep statistical data on their success and failures. Valid evaluation is the key to acquiring additional funding. Let's think of funders as investors. If early adopters have conducted a small but successful test of a teaching technique or program, they can use this statistical data to convince funders to invest in a larger project. The path to success is there, because not only can the early adopter show them a technique that works, but the school has also demonstrated it has the expertise, facilities, and technical support to make a larger project successful. However, teachers do not generally take research methods courses until their master's programs, but there are many excellent sources on the Internet that teachers can use to guide them. They can also find other schools who have done similar projects and ask if they will share their measurement instruments, surveys, questionnaires, or portfolio activities.

THE SECOND WAVE

The second wave of teachers to use technology is very different from early adopters. They represent a trend of sustainability and permanence. When they catch on, the trend is for real; if they reject it, then there is too much work, too much hype, or the new technology is not as effective as what they are doing now. If early adopters are high maintenance, the next wave is even more so. They are a much larger group of teachers, so there are more of them to accommodate with technological support, facilities, and equipment. They are less willing to work independently, have no patience to do problem solving, are more apt to request and expect support, and are less tolerant of equipment or program glitches. But they are an army, not one soldier, and have a broad, systemic effect on change.

Watching and fretting over early adopters is much different from orchestrating the technology of an entire school. That is where governing technology is a must. There needs to be a vision for the school in order to plan how to equip and service the entire infrastructure of classrooms and support areas. The second wave doesn't have the time for experimentation that early adopters have or the patience for looking around for resources, lessons, or curriculum. They look to the technology staff for immediate support; look to companies to provide easy-to-use, effective curricula and lessons; and then expect administrators to find a way to pay for everything.

TEACHERS WHO WILL NOT USE TECHNOLOGY

Teachers will not all use technology no matter what initiatives, bribes, or threats are put before them. The notion that all teachers will provide their students with a technology-rich environment is too much to expect and not realistic with the academic freedom allowed in the U.S. school system. The reality is that there will always be a gradient curve in how teachers will or will not use technology, ranging from absolutely never to every day. As for the ones who will not use technology, let them be. It is not always because they are timid with computers. Often, it is because they just don't want to teach that way. This should be factored into strategic planning and purchasing to prevent the small fraction of never adopters from anchoring or inhibiting the rest of the school in its path to technology integration.

SUMMARY

To keep innovation and outside funding happening, business managers must allow innovation to occur by providing encouragement, seed money, and technical and facility support to early adopters. They need to guide teachers toward exploring opportunities for professional development, electronic networking, and distance training like interactive Webinars and teleconferences. Early adopters are evangelists for innovation and require channels for spreading the word to other teachers. Electronic communication can flow through the barriers of walls and duties that usually separate teachers in the same school network just as the early Internet's listservs magically linked teachers nationally. The second wave of users will require more strategic planning and governance in order to be managed effectively. All of these teachers must have the freedom and support to experiment and to apply local solutions to local problems.

Chapter Four

The Other Stakeholders

The financial and regulatory control of schools comes from many different stakeholders. One could not imagine a parent, employee, state legislator, or federal agency wielding control or influence over income, policy, budgets, or expenditures of Microsoft, Yahoo!, or Apple. It would be harder still to imagine that a clerical worker would decide to make widgets in his or her office and ignore what the rest of the company was doing. However, that is just what early adopters were doing. But early adopters are just one of many groups of stakeholders making widgets. Managers of technology have to be diligent and watchful to foster productive encounters with stakeholders, because at least one stakeholder will always be making widgets.

Schools have so many stakeholders, layers of authority, and volumes of money coming from a variety of different directions such that management of finances, policies, and practices is tough, very tough, to stabilize. The financial whirlwind is governed by stakeholders, all of whom are able to make independent decisions, often with little knowledge of each other's actions. The degree of power that each has strengthens or weakens over time according to public opinion, strong individual personalities, and politics. One year, one stakeholder may be king of the hill; the next year, another can capture the flag and become king.

There is an interesting fact about the belief stakeholders have in their ability to improve schools—they all believe themselves to be experts in education. No one would like to try his or her hand at being a brain surgeon, a violinist, or a chemical engineer without training, practice, and acquisition of knowledge. However, most of the people who have survived the system of schools at any level consider their learning successes and experiences the right way for everyone. This makes stakeholders more apt to come up with absolutely wild plans to change the system to match their success. The common battle cry is "I learned by [phonetics, drill, field trips, memorization, singing, writing, listening, lecture, computers, games, hands-on learning, etc.], and to improve schools all children should learn this way."

Although most stakeholders are well meaning and sincere in their desire to improve education, this phenomenon of amateurs believing themselves to be experts and having power is difficult for educators. After all, they have the training, knowledge, and experience; however, a lawyer, insurance agent, scientist, plumber, or homemaker can have more say about policies, procedures, and funding in education than educators do. It can be a very hard pill for educators to swallow. Managers have to find ways to secure stakeholder funding while running the school as a business for education staffed by experts: local solutions for local problems.

Technology probably stirred the pot more than any other initiative because it affected every nook and cranny of schools and because each person in each nook and cranny had a strong opinion. It not only changed how work was done but altered and violated the physical space. Unlike televisions, slide projectors, and overheads more than one was needed in the room; hence, schools had to add new stakeholders, technology managers and technicians, into a system that had, understandably from previous battles of holding stakeholders at bay, built a fortification of resistance and reluctance to, sigh, add yet another stakeholder.

When doing complicated financial planning for schools, it is important to be able to anticipate and research from where money for technology may come, strategize about how to grab it, and budget accordingly, depending on whether the funds are permanent or windfalls. Managers also need to supplement those things that are not funded. Not all technology expenses will be attractive enough to lure sufficient funds. A stakeholder may give enough money to purchase thirty bright, shiny new computers in front of which the stakeholder and the students can have their picture taken for the newspaper but not fund the cost of rewiring the room and adding more electrical outlets for thirty computers. It is hard to impress anyone with a news photo of a funder pointing to an electrical outlet. This chapter will give an overall picture of the stakeholders, their rank, their likely amount of power in mandating policies or controlling budgets, and, most importantly, what types of financial gifts or burdens they bring to the table.

FEDERAL GOVERNMENT

Because there is more press about federal issues than about how the school down the street is managed, there is a false perception that schools are regulated nationally. The fact is that the constitution prevents the United States from having a national system of education. The programs that schools offer aim to ensure that every child in the United States has an equal opportunity for success and the resources for a high-quality education. However, every president wants to be known as *the* education president. Because education affects the majority of voters, it provides great campaign goodwill and PR. Each new president will use the power he or she has for an innovative initiative to improve schools. The result is that federal funds for schools will go toward whatever challenge the president wants to take. When a new president comes into office, schools are left scrambling to regroup so that they can compete in the new race in the area where the new money may fall.

Whatever the focus of the president, it must be within federal constitutional boundaries and address a current national concern. The federal government's control of schools is pretty much limited to ensuring that each state provides free and equal schooling and services to all children, hence the concentration on putting funds in places where they can equalize the quality of education. The money is distributed in many ways. Some is distributed through competitive grants for exemplary programs that address the presidential goal du jour. Other grants are formula grants for national initiatives, which give a piece of the pie to schools that fit a targeted demographic or profile. There are also earmarked projects in which a legislature manipulates money through various political connections and pathways. Most of these projects are worthy; some are a tad bit suspicious. The president can direct how much money is allotted through open competition, formula, and earmarks. Federal money always comes with a tangled web of attached strings and a price tag.

It would be reasonable to think that federal money would be easy to identify; it is not. Once found, it is not always easy to apply for. One cannot just scribble off a note saying "Please send money." Open competition means that someone has to not only write a grant but also do it well, because the competition among applicants is fierce. The grant must propose a project, justify why it will improve education, create a budget to show how the funds would be spent, and demonstrate that there are highly qualified people to manage the project. These grants can take up to a year to prepare. Grant writing is a highly skilled sport, and it is difficult but not at all impossible for schools without professional, trained, or experienced grant writers to compete.

Sometimes, more often under some administrations than under others, education funds can be acquired through clever and targeted networking with legislators and federal agencies. Funds can come from some surprising places by earmarking funds before they are up for competition or even formula funding. Earmarks are funds that are appropriated before they are open to competitive applications. To appropriate these funds, schools will employ lobbyists, if they are legal, or, if not, community-relations staff to work with legislators to make them aware of the needs of the school.

STATES

The bulk of the constitutional power for governing schools is given to the states. Each state sets up its governing board a little differently; however, usually the governor appoints a board of education that governs the educational policies and standards of the state. The board oversees operations via the state department of education, which in turn oversees activities like compliance with federal regulations, teacher certification, and distribution of state tax funds. Most states also have technology staff to oversee the state infrastructure.

Like the federal government, the states also control schools by tugging at their purse strings, either by threatening to withhold funds or by giving away funds. However, states have more strength to yank at the strings, since their money represents about 50 percent of a school's budget. This money comes from state taxes and federal allotments. State money for schools is a budget line item, but the amount is usually up for lively negotiation each year by the governor and/or legislators. They will determine the amount of money that will go directly to the schools' general operating funds and the amount that will be allocated for special projects like technology.

The legislature can also appropriate additional funding according to the needs of the schools, public requests, or the political climate. The states and special-interest groups all like to keep close to what is happening in the legislature. Sometimes appropriation is good, like when extra money was appropriated for wiring schools, but unfortunately extra money for one project means another one didn't get funded. There are always cheers and jeers after the state budget is finalized. The impact on schools is that each year they are challenged to regroup to follow the money. It is a tricky business, and they keep a close eye on legislative issues.

LOCAL SCHOOL DISTRICTS

The real power in the governance, management, and day-to-day support systems for running the schools lies with the local school districts. The districts are funded by local taxes, which represent about 40 percent of their revenue. The size and location of the districts are usually a geographical decision made by the local taxing area or legislators. Unfortunately, boundaries can expand, shrink, or wander with political issues, and they do. Generally, cities will have their own districts, and rural schools are commonly run by a county district. The leadership comes from a locally elected board that has power to hire a superintendent who, in turn, hires the rest of the administrators, teachers, and staff. The amount of control the board has and the degree of micromanaging it does depend on the current political climate and the power and skills of the superintendent. The board approves the budget and in some districts is also the body that draws it up.

The district provides support services and organization for all the schools. This usually includes services for maintaining a high quality of teaching and learning, like curriculum specialists, coordination of teacher training, and special projects like dual enrollment. They also provide coordination for student services, like counseling services and special needs programs. Also included are coordinated business services like record keeping and accounting services. For our purposes here, the most important service is the centralized control of information technology maintained by most districts.

LOCAL SCHOOLS

Each individual school is responsible for its own day-to-day management, although it must consider mandates from all of the above. The strength of individual schools lies in the academic freedom to choose how they teach and the constitutional power of the schools to reflect the needs and values of their communities. Each school takes on a personality of its own, which varies according to how management manages and teachers teach. With the help of technology, schools have the ability to cut through the federal, state, and district mandates, policies, and restrictive funding to address local problems and to innovatively make local solutions.

The principal, who may also be the business manager, is responsible for interpreting the rules from above, producing and following a budget, and overseeing teachers, service specialists, and support staff. He or she is responsible for much of the overall character of the school, its effectiveness, and the working environment. He or she has the most direct influence over teachers, especially the early adopters, and can choose to encourage them to pursue outside opportunities and funding or prohibit any type of individual activity.

The principal is also the gatekeeper for technology that will or will not be used in the schools and often decides who gets technology and who does not. Whether or not the district supplies technical support staff, the principal can budget additional support for the school. He or she can also decide upon the type of person that the school will hire for technical support: a teacher who likes technology, an ex-student fresh out of high school, or a trained technician with a college or technical school degree.

PARENTS

The strength, energy, and financial resources of the parents can make an incredible difference toward acquiring technology. A powerful parent organization or even one single parent can greatly impact what a school can or will be able to do. This can be just as easily a negative factor as a positive one. Parents can contribute time and resources for technology, like banding together to wire the school or getting their companies to donate computers. But they can just as easily throw their efforts into sports, buildings, or other special-interest programs. The money they produce is rarely a large sum and most often follows as long as they have children in the school. Surprisingly, the same parents are not as willing to support schools when they move to a retirement community.

LOCAL AND NATIONAL INDUSTRY AND BUSINESSES

The local business community has a stake in schools for many different reasons, many of which they profit from. The quality of local schools greatly impacts surrounding businesses and industry in many ways. For example, real-estate values are directly linked to the rating of the schools. The better the schools are, the higher the value of the houses in the service area. Schools are also important recruitment tools for local employers. Potential employees are looking for a good quality of life, and schools are a forerunner of that. It behooves industry to give money to keep the schools progressive and of high quality. The amount and sophistication of technology a school has are an important benchmark for a high-quality school.

Most companies set aside advertising dollars to create community goodwill. They want to fund projects that have their name prominently displayed. The funds that they provide range from small grants, for teachers to do little classroom projects, to large donations for buildings, technology labs, or sports stadiua. They prefer the large, splashy, and sexy projects, like a sports stadium that gets their name in the papers every Friday night. It is hard or impossible to get them to fund operating expenses.

Nationally, companies also want to use advertising money to create goodwill. Some will identify individual schools because they are part of an issue in which they are interested. These issues can be long-term or short-term. A company may make a long-term commitment to funding reading programs in underserved schools. Another company may be interested for a couple of years in reading education for minorities and then switch to a new focus on helping exemplary science students.

SUMMARY

There are many pros and cons to the stakeholders. As business managers govern, finance, and manage technology they have to be aware of, sometimes wary of, stakeholders. The good news is that the stakeholders bear gifts of cash or goods. The diversity of ways in which schools can obtain funds makes acquiring technology possible even without it being a line item on the budget. When technology threatens to break the budget, there are other sources of revenue to supplement the deficit, especially for initiatives that have shown success. The bad side is that the gifts are given by a rotating group of stakeholders who come and go, and decisions are often politically motivated.

Chapter Five

Managing the Stakeholders

The total number of stakeholders who have a say in financing schools is intimidating for business managers. It is also important that stakeholders bearing gifts of great cash be welcomed but not allowed to invade and occupy. Business managers need to be knowledgeable and sufficiently savvy in order to grab opportunities when they arise and employ tactics to temper the chaos. This allows them to gain financial control while still progressing and growing rather than watching opportunities fade away for lack of appropriate vision. On a national arena, systematic change is possible, but only on a geologic timeline (the time it takes to move a mountain) and not in real time, when schools need it. However, on a local level, there is a great deal of freedom that allows the system to be responsive to the needs of individual schools or districts and blissfully off the national radar. One school with wise and informed management can charge merrily along on its way to excellence. The larger national system will just grind away slowly at making change.

The key for business managers is to become informed about the larger system and make it work for the school. To do this, it is necessary to recognize what can be improved, what cannot be changed, and ways in which the system can be manipulated so that it can be used to an advantage, or at least be targeted for damage control when it gets in the way. This requires a thoughtful study of each influencing factor and analysis of the ways in which each can be contended with or managed.

THE REALITY OF STAKEHOLDERS

The multiple rowdy stakeholders are not going to be organized into one happy group of folks collectively working for a common cause. They may all be rallying behind a common theme, technology, but they are all going to participate and contribute differently. That is a good thing. Because of their unique cultural, social, economic, ethnic, family structure, geographical, and educational demographic mixes, schools have very different needs from each other. For example, a school in a remote Appalachian region may need satellite dishes to access the Internet because it is too expensive to lay cable over miles of country roads that wind around a ridge. A school in an affluent community may need money to purchase a digital projection system because it is building a planetarium on the rooftop. Another school with a changing student population and demographics may need money for language or reading labs. All of these scenarios show that schools must have opportunities to fund the projects that are right for their students—local solutions to local problems.

Technology is expensive, and business managers have to strategize on how it can be funded. Getting an increase in operating funds from stakeholders is one way of getting more money, but asking them to give more is difficult and slow. Schools have to decide if they will steal from the pie or bring in new money. This requires working with stakeholders and successfully arguing why the funds are needed, what will be done with them, and then proving that the funds accomplished what they set out to do. To gain additional funds to get technology started, schools need to seek grants or donations from any stakeholder with an open wallet; but first, keep two things in mind.

Remember that the best, most productive way to think of stakeholders is as investors. The money they give to education is an investment, not a gift without accountability. Like any investor, they want to see positive, productive results. They give money to a particular school when they have confidence in its ability to use the money wisely to solve a problem by the end of a program or to seed a project that will be sustained permanently by the administration. Lose this confidence and the school will lose the funder. Expect that they will ask the school to perform a formative, ongoing evaluation that guides the project to reach its goals and a summative evaluation to show its successes and continued challenges. This evaluation will require, from day one, a collection of both qualitative (hard statistics) and quantitative (testimonials or observational) data.

Next, no one wants to invest in a loser. In the 1960s, it was oh-so-popular to invest in struggling grassroots organizations staffed by overambitious, well-meaning do-gooders. Investors would empty their pockets to keep alive an organization with a noble goal. That is not so today. Investors want to fund exemplary projects, not those that might wilt and wither away after the funding is spent. They also want to see success. If a school says it needs technology for a math program to bring students up to the state passing level, they want to see this achieved. They will want to review project budgets and know how the school operated within them. That is a predominate reason why some schools or teachers always get grants and others do not.

LOCATING FEDERAL FUNDS

The bulk of federal funds for schools come from the Department of Education. A good portion goes directly to the state education department, which is responsible for dividing funds up amongst their schools. But there are many ways in which individual schools or districts can compete on their own for additional funds. The most important way for business managers to organize this hunt for funding is to remember that this is a group sport, and a healthy working relationship and camaraderie are key. The state will have specialists who keep abreast of federal funds and will distribute information to districts and schools, but it certainly helps for a business manager to build a personal relationship with state department of education folks to speed up and direct the information flow.

It is also paramount for the information to flow in two ways. As schools apply for and pursue federal funds, they should inform the appropriate state and district authorities about what they are doing before they do it. This prevents conflicts with other schools and districts or the state's grants and other initiatives. It can also help to find a partner. The state agency may spot a good match with another school that has similar goals. Partnering usually strengthens the likelihood of winning a grant or funding, increases the money, shares the administration costs, and broadens the scope of what can be done. It is beneficial for all parties.

The school's senators and representatives can help identify likely federal funds, lobby the funding agency, and even negotiate for direct or earmark funds, which will bypass a lengthy grant application. Again, the state office of education keeps in close contact with them, so keeping state officials in the loop is important. When working with senators or representatives, they will need to know what the school's needs are, what facts and figures justify the requested funds, and how the funding will improve the school or district. Everyone wins here. Elected officials like to know how they can help the people that elected them to office, especially since they will need their support again come next election day. They, in turn, can pave the way for better funding.

Build a personal relationship with them and their staff. Most live half the year or more in Washington, D.C., but they do have local staff whose sole job is to keep in contact with constituents. Technology here is a must. It generates an automatic way to keep connected. Send invitations to special events, graduations, visits to exemplary classrooms, and informal information sessions. E-mail all the school's newsletters and press releases, and include lists of graduates, students who have won scholarships, athletes, student leaders, and so on. Brag as well as beg. This will help them become more informed so that when they go to Washington they can identify opportunities and funds that will help your school and negotiate for the school's proposals.

The process of writing and applying for grants is similar for most federal agencies. The agency's project administrators and officers will identify a problem or area in which they want to target their funds. It could be they want to provide computers to underfunded, lower socioeconomic schools, they may want to get more high-achieving students into computer technology, or they may want elementary students to use computers to help boost reading skills. Once they decide, they will then issue an announcement, an RFP (Request for Proposal), that explains the goal and desired outcomes, states what qualifications would make a school eligible, and gives instructions on how to apply. There will also be a hard and fast due date with no exceptions, except of course if the school is very good at building relationships.

After the due date, grants will be submitted to a review panel, which usually consists of program officers, past grant recipients, and knowledgeable professionals in the field. The reviewers will read and rate each grant, usually on a point system based on a rubric, which will rank them anywhere from rejected to recommend. Recommends will go to the grant officer or officers for consideration. Not all of the recommends receive funding, because there are always more great grants than cash. It is often the federal program officers, administrators, and amount of money available that determine exactly what grants from the favored pile will actually be funded.

The robustness, feasibility, and creativeness of the idea of how the school is going to solve a problem are always the tipping point for what wins the grant. However, a good idea alone without a solid plan of implementation won't tip anything. The idea must clearly and simply identify a specific situation or problem the grant wants to address (remember, local solutions for local problems), suggest a solution that will make an improvement in student learning, and provide a plan of how it will be accomplished. It then needs to be stressed why the school's situation is important and—extremely critical—why it is important to fund your school rather than another. Finally, even thought it may be a local problem, how would what the school learns about solving the problem apply to other schools with similar situations across the country? If you have a new electronic reading program and teaching method for students who do not get reading support at home, can another school with similar demographics also successfully use your findings to increase their scores?

Build a case documented by the education literature or pilot tests in the school. For example, if the school wants to purchase notebook computers for all the math classes to provide students with more and immediate feedback, it will be necessary to defend why notebook computers or that teaching method would improve math scores. Have other schools used different or similar methods successfully? Does using notebooks or that teaching method build on what other schools have found? What new or innovative programs or software will the students be using? Have other teachers used a similar program with the target population that would suggest to you that your idea would work? What from the literature suggests that your project will be unique?

The most challenging part is to provide reviewers with the statistics that show that the homework has been done and that the grant team has quantitatively identified the correct problem. This is where technology helps. The data that computers are able to collect and make readily available—data like attendance records, grade level grades, individual class grades, SAT scores, and student attrition—can identify problems that individual schools have. For example, the school's students are not passing the sixth-grade exit exams at the same rate as other students in the state. Identify exactly what level and conditions are possible causes and design your program to begin there. Are students starting to fall behind in math at the fourth, fifth, or sixth grade? Are students doing fine in the lower math skills but struggling in pre-algebra readiness and solving word problems? What are the attendance and attrition when the decline seems to start? Are certain ethnic or socioeconomic groups doing worse or better than others are? Are individual teachers better at preparing students, and what teaching methods are they using? You can provide lots of supportive evidence.

Next, check whether students are doing the same, better, or worse than those in other schools with similar demographics are. The Department of Education National Center for Education Statistics hosts a Web site that provides national statistics that enable schools to find benchmarks—how other schools nationally or with similar demographics are faring.[1] If the national average of math scores is fifty and the school's is thirty, then the goal may be to raise math scores to fifty over a three-year period by using an improved teaching technique with notebook computers. If your school's score is sixty, then explain how the funding agency will find your proposal more necessary than one at a school with an average score of thirty. Their need seems to be greater. You may want to alter your idea by partnering with another school with lower scores, by focusing on the students that are not doing well, or by investigat-

---

1. National Center for Educational Statistics, www.ed.nces.gov.

ing and publishing why your students are doing so well. Give your idea a twist that will solve not only your problem but a national one.

How is the school going to manage the grant? The plan needs to explain in detail exactly how the school will implement the program. This includes a description of key personnel who will be involved, their qualifications, and how they will fit this into their regular duties or how the school will provide extra or buy-out time. What resources will the school provide and how might it do so? How will the technology staff accommodate sixty or more students using laptops, and how will the facilities staff handle the increased intranet users, provide wireless connections, and install software? Unlike nontechnology grants, teachers cannot write these grants alone; they need support and guidance from the technology staff. Technology staff must be part of the grant plan.

An evaluation plan has to be built. This is the age of accountability for schools, and they have to quantitatively and qualitatively show progress. Continued and future funding relies heavily on statistics that prove the grant was managed properly and achieved the intended results. If the grant did not achieve the intended results, an informed explanation that identifies why the results were not realized and what measures were taken to adapt the plan to develop a successful formula is needed. For large grants, the evaluation could cost as much as 10 percent of the total amount. It is always wise to have a professional evaluator help write the plan. Many do this in exchange for their employment if the grant is funded.

Writing federal grants is not an overnight process. There is never enough time, so ways have to be found to expedite the writing process without losing quality. Treat it as a group sport. It usually takes a committee of people to formulate the idea, gather statistics, write the grant, create the budget, and complete the application. This blend of talents and training needs management, but technology can also help with this. Project management software, file sharing, and other software can be used to communicate electronically between the grant writers, budget developers, and staff entering figures. Teacher isolation is very real, but teachers have embraced e-mail to break that isolation. Use this to your advantage. Teachers can work on their portions of the grant during planning time, after school, or at home.

Most of the federal application processes are now online at www.grants.gov. Each person can work on his or her portion and input it directly onto the grant Web site. The teachers can work on the narrative, the secretary on the demographic information, the technology staff on the support plan, and the evaluator on his or her section. The budget portions even add up the columns to make sure the addition is correct. When the grant is complete, just a push of the button submits it.

NETWORKING WITH PROGRAM OFFICERS

When potential programs are identified, the next step is to sign up for electronic newsletters and updates that will automatically be sent out with information about new programs, changes in the regulations, or goals. Each funding area has one or too many program officers whose job is to work with applicants to help them be a success before they get passed on to the independent reviewers, who will make the final recommendations. The program officer cannot ethically tell you if you have a winning grant. He or she can, however, guide you to the issues that are important to the agency, what the background of the readers of the grant may be, the best writing style, and provide other suggestions he or she feels are appropriate. The program officer can also be your advocate.

The first and best way to reach program officers is by e-mail. The next best way to network with them is a bit more expensive but very effective, and that is to attend the training workshops held throughout the country to prepare schools to write the grant. Finally, volunteer as a program reviewer. This is a double win. Reviewers have the opportunity to network with the program officer, but also learn while reading the other grants how other schools formulated their ideas. It is not surprising that reviewers turn into successful grant writers.

NETWORKING WITH SUCCESSFUL GRANT WRITERS

Technology makes it easy to communicate with those who have written and administered successful grants. Almost every agency has a list of the winners of the last rounds who have Web sites that describe the grant and its progress or final report. As much as everyone would like to think that their grant idea is unique, there is probably another school that has tackled the same or a similar problem, like using technology to improve math scores, or taken a similar path, like using notebook computers rather than paper and pencil tasks. Via e-mail, contact the grant managers, evaluators, and participants for advice and assistance. Keep them in mind as outside evaluators or consultants to help you both write and administer your grant.

PARTNERING

Partnering is a way to increase the chances of winning a grant. It is a way of getting someone else to work for the school. Universities, four-year colleges, and community colleges are always seeking collaborators for their projects, and most federal grants require some type of partnership with a school or district both locally and nationally. The advantage to the school is that university professors have abundant resources at hand for grant writing. Professors, especially those in or pursuing tenure-track positions, are expected to write and win grants. They have a professional and monetary stake; that is a good thing for your side.

Informal educational organizations like museums, zoos, and nature centers also qualify for federal grants, and they too need partners to strengthen their position. They could provide special on-site classes or exhibits that will boost student interest or enthusiasm in subjects. They can also provide students with hands-on experiences by teaching using real objects that would otherwise not be offered in public schools. Touching elephant skin, examining thousand-year-old spear points, or interacting with robot dinosaurs are things that schools will never be able to do, but museums can bring these types of adventures to a school.

Most informal educational institutions like museums are old hands at providing online resources for schools and students. Early on, the NSF (National Science Foundation) gave them, along with formal educational institutions, public and private colleges, high schools, and elementary schools, free use of the Internet. The Genetic Science Learning Center (GSLC) was an example of a university, museum, and state board of education partnership grant. The university administered the grant. The large benefits to Utah schools were the free resources and teacher workshops. Teachers were able to earn in-service credit for workshops, some of which were conducted at the Eccles Institute of Genetics, and the lecturers were name researchers and pioneers in genetic research.

Community centers, youth organizations, and libraries can extend the reach of the school because they can interact with students outside of the regular school day. As seen with pilot testing of Exploring Life (EL), students who do not have home access to computers rely on these resources. Many underserved students have ethnic centers, youth organizations, and churches that supply people and resources. The trend in the current administration of granting money to faith-based organizations opened an entire new resource for funding. This may not entirely disappear when a new president is elected.

Universities, colleges, and community colleges have education faculty who seek federal funds to investigate new and innovative ways for teaching. EL partnered with Lehigh University's education department to organize the evaluation that fed the development of the program. The benefits to schools were teacher professional development, travel money to conferences and focus groups, and use of the EL program. Also, don't stop with the education departments. Most science and math faculty who receive federal funds for research or other projects have an education component attached to their funding. They need to partner with a school or school district.

THE FORMULA FOR SUCCESS FOR FEDERAL GRANTS

It is not the intent of this chapter to give a course in grant writing. The intent is to impress upon the reader how large a project writing federal grants can be and the importance of a good manager to direct the project. Admittedly, schools with professional grant writers fare better than those who are inexperienced or who do not or cannot invest in a grant writer. But professional grant writer or not, the key ingredient is the manager. Grant writing teams need the business manager to be a leader who is a good organizer, cheerleader, and bean counter to organize the search for the grants, assemble the teams, and push the submit button on time.

- Organize a grant team. Identify teachers who can clearly define a problem and design a plan to solve it. Instruct administrative and front-office support people who are familiar with the school's database to gather appropriate data to verify the problem. This data will serve as a benchmark for the evaluative plan. Identify a person to create a proposed budget that is realistic for the needs of the project.
- Use partnerships to avoid the sole responsibility of writing or administering the grant. Will a university or informal educational institution bring more resources and expertise to the program? For example, a grant for curriculum design will benefit from a partnership with a state museum that has scientists and Web designers on staff.
- Follow the directions. The grant needs to be written in an interesting style to keep the reviewers, who are facing a mountain of grants to read, energized. But they will quickly—whoa, you can't believe how quickly—eliminate a grant when they can't find the information on their checklist. They don't forgive, they toss. This list is generated by the program offices that created the proposal guidelines, so they know it well and are looking for an excuse to weed down the amount of reading they will have to do from hundreds of proposals to tens.
- Rewrite and resubmit. If your grant is rejected but received good reviews, rewrite it according the comments the reviewers have provided and resubmit it to that agency or to another. The persistent prevail. Plus, you save time, energy, and resources by improving what you have already written. It is not uncommon for grants to be resubmitted many times until the writing, idea, and implementation plan are improved.
- Let technology work for you. Have the front-office staff make an accessible database of information that all grants require so that teachers, staff, and administrators can easily access the information and plug it into grants they are writing. Items to include are a description of the school complete with

demographic statistics, a list of grants that are in the application process and those that are funded, and

- Experience helps and it gets easier. Old grants can be rewritten according to reviewers' comments to strengthen them. Never give up. One grant had been submitted nine times before it was funded. It began with a three-hundred-thousand-dollar budget and was funded at two million. The problem in the beginning was that it was a great idea, but the grant writers had not asked for enough money to do the project well. It took many tries to get the operational plan solidified.

STATE FUNDING

States hold the largest of the purse stings and need the closest watching by schools. That is because they are, like the federal government, subject to political swings. Most state departments of education keep a watchful eye on politics throughout the year, during the legislative sessions, and as the governor's budget is being debated. They are looking for the whole educational pie, while the individual districts and schools, fork in hand, are looking for a big slice of the pie. Schools can help the state educators by keeping their state representatives and senators informed about their achievements and unique educational needs. Put them on e-mail lists for newsletters, press releases, and other good news. Invite them or their staff to special functions. Provide them with lists of graduates, students who earn scholarships, science-fair winners, children who achieve attendance awards, and so on.

Under the watchful eye of the federal government, funds that states receive are divided somewhat equally among schools, and you just have to wait for the announcement of what the school's share is. However, there are special funds that are earmarked for targeted projects, like providing extra money to low-achieving or lower socioeconomic schools for a project that some stakeholder has proclaimed or been convinced will improve education. States also have extra money or programs for teacher professional development targeting early adopters or master teachers. In all cases, they rely on the schools communicating their needs to them. The Internet and e-mail are important and time-efficient ways to do so.

PRIVATE FUNDERS

Private funders have much the same requirements as the federal government. However, there is an interesting difference: they want to date. They require a relationship before they invest money, because they are using their money to establish community or national goodwill. Putting pins on a map to show the extent of their outreach is of great interest to them. They want to touch as many areas as they possibly can and naturally want a wide-ranging reach. Other funders prefer to fund schools in districts where they have branches, offices, or plants. They are looking to sustain or improve the quality of life in areas in which they have employees. For a person weighing an employment offer either to move or not to move away, having a technologically rich school for their children is high on the checklist. Other companies prefer to fund projects that target a specific demographic, socioeconomic group, age, scholastic level, or ethnicity. Many companies have think tanks, often consisting of their own employees, which identify and target a specific need and design projects that will aid

What most private funders don't want to do is give money directly to schools or districts in any way that could be construed as operating costs, or money could be lost or diluted in the quagmire of general operating funds. They prefer to fund an entire separate project and clearly define how money will be spent. They prefer to give to a person or group of people with a clearly defined plan and a history of good work. Capitalize on early adopters, because they are gold. Early adopters will canvas the world to find ways to get the money to do what they want. The same early adopters, their converts, and new educators entering the system will stumble on grants and are happy to pass along tips. They are avid users of listservs and discussion groups and have their own private e-mail network of people they meet at conferences, at national and local workshops, and by reading professional publications.

SUMMARY

Stakeholders all have money. It is up to the business manager to make sure the school takes control to attract and keep their attention. Individual schools have a great deal of freedom and encouragement to apply for outside funding. This is important money because it gives schools the ability to have extra funds to supplement national, state, or commercial textbooks and materials that do not solve local problems. But in order to apply for these grants, business managers need to set up the school for success by communicating and networking with funders, establishing a visual professional identity of accomplishment and achievement, and effectively coordinating the grant proposal writing. When grants are won, business managers need to ensure that the grant is administered as promised, that evaluations are conducted properly, and that the results are disseminated to promote both the school and the funder.

Chapter Six

The Path of Getting Computers into the Classroom

Although the publicity about the acquisition of technology for education was about classroom use, computers actually took a long time to get into the classrooms and still haven't completely made it. As technology entered schools, there were two factors that influenced where it was placed. One was that technology was financially tethered by the cost of laying cable, so computers were placed at the end of an affordable string. The other was that those who had a convincing argument and a very specific, well-defined task with achievable goals attracted stakeholders' money and got computers first. Early on, the central office and the library won on both of these counts and were able to progress steadily, albeit haphazardly, toward their goals of growing, refining, and completing their technology packages.

It is important for business managers to take note that optimizing student learning is not just a matter of placing computers in the classroom. It includes investigating and improving ways to diagnose, assess, and track students and designing appropriate teaching strategies. It includes training students in job-related skills: basic computer applications like word processing, publishing, writing and editing, spreadsheets, mixing and editing music, creating visuals, and illustrating, all of which are skills students must have in order to use the content they have learned. It includes having students become proficient in information management by using research skills and learning how to find information, evaluate its validity, and apply it to problem solving. It also demonstrates that technology is not just for school hours but includes extracurricular activities and access to school before and after official hours. Finally, it includes adapting teaching techniques to meet the restrictions of the teaching environment as well as the needs of the students.

The first computers connected to the Internet were commonly in the central office. The stakeholders, state agencies, districts, and schools had a reason for computers going there: record keeping. It was also affordable without miles of cable, the need was defined, and efficient data collection attracted stakeholder money. Schools could enter data via the Internet to the district or state offices. Computers made it an easy task to enter and organize data that was once handwritten, haphazardly collected, and often perilously preserved. It was easily transformed into quick-to-produce, reliable, and valuable statistics. Schools purchased office computers, auxiliary equipment, and software with money from the state or district offices that stipulated the exact model of the computers, software, and equipment that the school had to buy. This made purchasing simple and easy.

Teachers, being teachers, did march students into the secretary's office to use the Internet, but the central office was not an ideal learning place for students. One can just imagine the horror of the clerical staff person as excited students crowded around his or her desk intent on seeing something on the Internet. Although the central office is not good for student use, it is a great place for tracking and reporting student statistics to the district or state offices. This became a value added for business managers as data became more easily collected, archived, and analyzed.

Computers make it easier for clerical staff to track both quickly and efficiently such statistics as attendance, tardiness, and students who actually eat lunch instead of squandering money on snacks. One click and a teacher, nurse, counselor, or principal can see the average attendance rate of a student, a classroom, a grade level, or the entire school. Menus could be compared to lunch count to learn what meals are most popular or what food needs to be re-ordered. Although it may not seem obvious how some of this improves student learning, these statistics sound alarms when students' behavior changes. A student suddenly not eating, one persistently late for class unexpectedly, or a classroom of students with growing absenteeism becomes an early alert system for at-risk intervention.

With the secretary's patience exhausted, and with more technology money trickling in but way short of what was needed for computers for every classroom, it became obvious that schools needed a common place where students would have easier access than crawling over the secretary's desk. Putting thirty computers in one classroom would not work because students would not have equal opportunities. The library fit the bill. Libraries had extended hours before and after school. Teachers were already accustomed to sharing and reserving the facilities. The librarians had experience managing media centers with tape recorders, slide projectors, movie projectors, televisions, and VCRs. They were trained to use the Internet, and they had a national network, infrastructure, and outside professional support organizations and standards that were independent of the schools. This made the library the next target for cable, wires, and technology.

Librarians had a head start in using technology because electronic databases happened as quickly as computers appeared and librarians could type them in. Transforming print databases into electronic format had immediate rewards: efficiency and speed increased, they were easier to maintain, and they cost less to manage. However, the first computers in libraries were slow and clunky, some bigger than a washing machine, and, like an exposed nerve, they were temperature sensitive. They used fragile reels of tape or even more fragile floppy disks. Only large or lucky libraries could afford them. These databases on disk could be mailed to smaller libraries; however, updates were infrequent and happened not when information changed but when libraries could afford to mail tapes or disks.

The Internet and personal computers (PCs) allowed even the smallest, remotest, or poorest libraries to have access to databases. Before Mosaic, libraries used the Internet via a program called FTP (File-Transfer Protocol), an application that downloaded files from other computers. The resources were text-rich materials and the users a text-tolerant group. When the colorful Internet browsers arrived, they were value added and a grand kickoff for popular use of the Internet by the general public. Unlike electronic curriculum, libraries had already established a solid foundation in technology and were ready to go. Libraries became popular, even cool, as more powerful computers with high-speed connections to the Internet became available. With each new windfall, librarians just added more computers, pushing back the bookshelves and expanding the computer space.

At first, teachers believed that the library computers were an ideal venue for lessons, and at first, with just early adopters, that was feasible. The Internet and Web browsers changed that. Over time, as the libraries increased their access to electronic databases, e-journals, and e-books on fast computers, their clientele of students and teachers grew exponentially. The library's mission is information management, and librarians could not accommodate classrooms full of students monopolizing the computers for a lesson. Besides, as the early majority started using computers, it just got too crowded. Librarians needed their computers for their business. The last thing they wanted was a class of biology students taking the space of those they were to serve, students and teachers searching for and managing information. Like the front office staff, librarians quickly discovered that sharing their computers with teachers who wanted to do classroom lessons was just plain annoying. The classroom teachers were kicked out.

What proved to be highly advantageous about technology in the library was that it gave more opportunities for students to have access to electronic materials on their own. The library is an important access point for students who have inadequate or no access at home to do homework or extra activities. Teachers found that assigning computer activities is like assigning any research project in which students have to use books or databases for research. Libraries are open before and after school, during lunch, and during other open periods. These open periods were essential for student access. It was not the only place they could access computers, but it was an important one. Almost all the students, computer at home or not, could do the activities if they had a couple of days in which to complete them.

The drumming out of teachers and students wanting to use the library caused another round of funding to string more cable to another location in the school. This time the facilities would coincide with the mission of teachers using them for curriculum and lessons: no sharing with areas that had their own missions. Again, the problem was how to give teachers equal access. The solution was to put a classroom set of computers in a dedicated room where teachers could share the room to use electronic materials. The computer lab was born.

The labs were often a donated or commandeered classroom rearranged with salvaged tables tightly packed together into neat rows. With the exception of the compact Macintosh, computers then were massive machines. When thirty students, backpacks, chairs, printers, LCD (Liquid Crystal Display) projectors, and computers were added, there was no room for movement. Electronic materials woven into lessons require a variety of student and teacher interactions including group instruction, discussion, or giving directions to students distracted by gossip. Eye contact is important. It was easy for students to use the tightly packed computers to break contact with that evil eye of discipline. In a computer lab, no matter where the teacher roams, eye contact cannot be held with all students.

The normal noise level of thirty computers running often leaves the teacher standing in the front of the room screaming in order to be heard in the back. In an attempt to eliminate as much noise as possible and to avoid distraction, the computers in most labs don't have sound. This does little to help the teacher maintain student attention; the hum of the computers and LCD projectors is still overwhelming. The omission of sound eliminates the effectiveness of interactive tools that use audio to deliver material to students who learn by listening or use sound as a way of engaging and guiding students through activities. Besides, sound is enjoyable, keeps students interested, and is an effective way for students to learn. In the insane idea that reading is everything, this is forgotten. Students do learn by lecture, the sound of someone talking, and the ability to ask questions.

Another problem occurred—computer labs were hard to reserve. When the system caught up with training teachers to use technology, teachers wanted to use it. Computer labs became so booked that teachers found they had to reserve them a month in advance. What happened in most schools is that the disciplines that could best utilize a computer-lab environment had priority to use them for word processing and publishing software. Teachers were a tad miffed, especially when the statistical probability of actually doing a planned lesson on an appointed day was low. Even if they had a secure scheduled day, there was no guarantee they could get in. Snow days, assembly days, testing days, picture days, bad Internet days, and so on threw the schedule completely off. The mix of special days and technology disruptions is unpredictable. It is like playing Russian roulette with the curriculum.

Teachers have deadlines by which to complete lessons to ensure that everything that is required to be covered in a school year does. They have allotted time periods to complete topics and go on to the next. Even when deadlines are flexible, equal access for all the classes needs to be guaranteed. For example, a teacher planned on having the students read about photosynthesis in the classroom and then the next day use the lab to do the accompanying activity. An unscheduled assembly canceled morning classes resulting in those students missing the activity. Since the lab was booked for the rest of the month, the morning students missed out completely, but the afternoon students did not. Now there are two classes that have to take a test when only one completed the important reinforcing activity. If the classes get too uneven in experiences and content, it won't work. This is the age of accountability for schools. Teachers are responsible for students passing state exams and are under the gun to be sure the state core curriculum is covered by the appointed test date. The curriculum must flow smoothly and equally for all students.

In order for teachers to use technology in shared spaces, scheduling has to be dependable, reliable, and fair to all students. Most persons remember the droning, mind-numbing routine of school. For students, an unexpected departure from it is a gift from the gods. What students don't see, however, are teachers crazily scrambling around to sustain and foster that dull routine. Routine is the way in which teachers survive; otherwise, chaos rules in schools. Teachers can adjust if a disruption happens occasionally and randomly—eventually it will come out even in the end. Scheduling a computer lab can ruthlessly endanger the routine if something goes wrong, and it will.

Travel time is another reason that shared computer labs don't work when teachers have to follow schedules. The travel time that is necessary for students to go from classroom to lab takes away from instruction time. For example, two science teachers on block schedules decided to share a lab room. Block schedules are extended class periods of around two hours, give or take fifteen minutes in either direction. They can become a complicated schedule in which on blue days, students go here, and on gold days, students go there. The advantage of the long periods is that teachers have more time for laboratory exercises, class discussion, and hands-on activities. All of these are valuable learning experiences, but it is time-sapping to prepare materials and then coordinate them with the students.

The observed school was no different from others in that computer labs were hard to reserve, so the physics and math teacher decided to share a block period. The first forty-five minutes was for physics, and the second forty-five minutes was for biology. In her classroom, the biology teacher introduced the students to the new concepts, explained the activity they would be doing, and then led the march to the computer lab. This particular school was very large, and it took about seven minutes to herd everyone out to the hall, make the bend to the next corridor, tromp down the stairs, hike across the lunch area, and file quietly through the library to get to the labs. This is where the real bottleneck started.

The biology students began to sprint through the door at the same time the physics students were trying to stroll out. The students leaving were in no hurry, while the biology students, knowing which computers were best positioned to get all their buddies together, were eager to play a merry game of musical chairs. Then traffic stopped. It was never observed exactly what the landmass was that clogged the students coming and going, but it was always visualized as four students, arms and legs weaving, tightly wedged in the doorway. No one was going anywhere until the teachers unraveled the trapped students.

A class period is not the same as instruction time. When calculating the time available for activities and lessons, the actual instruction time is ten to fifteen minutes less than the class period. If the bell rings at 1:15, students have to be in the room at that time, not seated at their desks with pens poised to take notes. It is a skilled and really lucky teacher who can get a room settled down within the first five minutes of class. Part of the dull routine everyone endures is designed to get students working as quickly as possible without wasting a precious minute. Add travel time to the computer lab, and the amount of time for learning shortens even more.

Firing up the computer lab requires even more time. Some schools ask that students log into their accounts. To do this, one observed class had to boot up the computer, then log on. It seems a simple, quick task, but it eats into precious instruction time and adds another five minutes to getting everyone together for an activity. At the end, everyone has to take the time to log off. It takes seconds, but students shave off minutes, knowing there is another task to do before the mad dash to the next class.

In one pilot test, these factors led many teachers who did not have classroom computers and had to use computer labs to have difficulty completing the pilot tests. The curriculum integrated computers into everyday lessons, and using shared computer labs was not a good fit. The travel time for students, lack of just-in-time availability, and inconsistencies of reliability and access caused some, but not all, teachers to drop out of the testing. Some teachers, bribing or bullying for dates, did complete the testing using the labs. They were resourceful and adjusted the activities to fit by finding ways to have a regularly scheduled day for computer activities. Some, resigned that the lab schedule would always be inconsistent and smartly realizing that this was a constant, became shameless opportunists. They used the activities as reinforcement or review rather than as sequential activities paced with the text. If they missed a day, they good-naturedly chalked it up as a loss and hoped the next day would be better. Basically, they made it work.

There were additional problems beyond the shared computer rooms, because what was on the computers had to be shared also. Early on during the pilot tests, it became way too apparent that, like bad hair days, there were going to be bad Internet days, so the teachers were provided with a CD of the Web site. The students would not be able to access all of the activities, but most of the interactive activities, assessments, and readings were intact. In theory, this appeared to be a good remedy, until teachers were observed going into emergency mode. Thirty computers efficiently used meant thirty CDs. It is back to a time thing. CDs have to be passed out and collected. Students got a late start and had to end early.

Some teachers tried to install the program on the computers, but they were so stuffed full of other programs that there was not an inch of room left. In other cases, system managers protected the computers from the onslaught of teachers and students loading programs by installing blocks to prevent unauthorized uploads. Some system administrators allowed programs to be installed but wiped them out at the end of the day. It became an endless cycle of load, reload, load, reload. To technical developers, uploading a program doesn't sound like a lengthy task. For the teachers, it is. Thirty computers, thirty bored and completely rambunctious students, and one CD to upload the program was not a winning mix

Computer labs are good for a different type of teaching and learning strategy because labs restrict student movement and activities. To be successful in a computer lab, a program has to allow students to work independently from each other at their own pace alone with the computer—blissful for some. This is extremely effective for skill building, like learning how to type and use basic word-processing software. Keyboarding was an activity that worked well in labs. Students practice and build skills independently; there is little interaction and exchange of information between skill builders. They work productively like this the entire class period. The teachers' job is to keep students on task, not to referee lively activities or orchestrate free-thinking activities. Think of guitarists. They do not pick up a guitar and play in front of an applauding audience; they practice, all alone, for hours.

SUMMARY

The central office had a clear goal of providing diagnostic data for business managers and teachers. Data collection always had an obvious purpose—to support learning—but technology made it more important, an integrated part of education. Data provides information. That information can tell a parent if their child is in trouble or tell a business manager if a teacher is in trouble. The task for business managers is to make that information useful and accessible to teachers and support staff. Teachers need a hand in determining what information they need to know.

Labs were an economical way to arrange computers, but they had to fit within the constraints of old facilities—not an easy trick. Teachers shared the labs, giving all students some experience and practice over the school year. This *did* provide all students with some experience, but it was not a daily experience, a regular part of classroom routine, nor anywhere near the time or practice needed for inquiry or reflective problem solving activities. At the beginning of the introduction to technology, the important skill students needed was keyboarding: learning how to use basic application software and conquering the physical dexterity required for typing. To gain a high degree of skill, the students needed to be chained to the computer to practice, practice, and practice just as if they were learning the piano or violin. That worked well in one large room that was stuffed with computers and had absolutely no room in which to move around. In these labs, students learn how to use computers, not how to learn with computers.

That being said, not all of the teachers abandoned the use of shared lab facilities. The reality is that not all schools are going to be able to purchase and then support computers in every classroom. The next chapter describes what teachers and administrators did to accommodate the challenges they had. They not only faced the practical task of getting computers to the students in the classroom but also confronted the learning model of every student needing to have his or her own computer in a neat row.

Chapter Seven

The Perfect Learning Environment

The title of this chapter is kind of tongue-in-cheek. There is not a single model for one perfect learning environment, which is very unfortunate because it would be a great economic boost to education to have that one-size-fits-all education solution. The perfect learning environment is a creative and thoughtful arrangement and mix of teaching tools that surpass budget and facility restrictions. Technology is a tool for teaching and a venue and an instrument for learning. Placed in various spaces, classrooms, and labs and used by a variety of software and hardware, technology can be used in distinctive ways to adapt to various teaching strategies. Different subject matter requires unique types of activities and room settings. The task of business managers is to mediate and arbitrate among teachers, facilities managers, and technical staff to fit learning with the environment and teaching goals of a teacher, school, or district.

The value of the diverse stakeholders' goals and the spontaneity of when they came through with money was that it allowed schools an opportunity to experiment with learning environments. Teachers dragged in one, five, or twenty computers, lined them up or piled them up, partnered with developers or made their own lessons, and then watched as students used them. With the next round of funding, they tweaked the successful combinations or abandoned those that did not work for their situation.

Most Internet sources are Web sites that supplement the curriculum; they are not the curriculum. An explanation: the curriculum is all of the daily lessons that comprise the learning objectives for the entire course, which usually extends over a year. On the Internet or in other resources, teachers found the materials they wanted and could fit them, at any time and in any way, into lessons. Occasional or supplemental lessons make it easy for a teacher to adjust his or her daily lesson plans to meet the scheduling restrictions of the computer labs, exchange rooms with another teacher, or reserve the roving LCD projector in order to do the activity. A bad technology day is highly annoying but not deadly for the curriculum. This does not hold true for programs that comprise of a year's worth of lessons into a curriculum that weaves in the unique qualities of technology.

As information came in from those years, it was obvious that teachers were struggling to match the physical design of classrooms and other facilities with the activities, and it was a mismatch that was not easy to fix. There was general surprise about the concessions and compromises teachers had to make and the creativity required to craft an engaging, technology-rich environment. Teachers migrated from place to place, changing this and moving that, in order to try to make do with what they had. This experimentation and flexible thinking was all part of the loosely scientific process of building models for creating learning environments. As in scientific research, failure was an important and contributing part of this progression, to the frustration of teachers.

The original instructional model that early adopters and developers envisioned was that each student would have his or her own computer. Throughout the class period, students could access lessons as they moved from textbook to computer interactives and lab to computer data entry and analysis. Activities lasted for ten, fifteen, thirty, or forty minutes and required much movement. Early adopters went through many trials trying to produce this model. In theory, every student having his or her own computer is ideal; it is just great. However, teachers largely found that it does not fit into what schools can physically accommodate, nor does it match the best way for students to learn.

When early integration began, government figures reported that over 80 percent of schools and almost 50 percent of instruction rooms had Internet access. This, like most statistics, needs explaining. The ratio of computers to students was nine to one, which sounds good until you do the numbers. In a school of five hundred students that meant there were fifty or so computers, total, for student use. This is two classroom sets, hardly enough to provide each student during each class period with a technology-rich learning environment.

The responses from the field-tester applications from the Exploring Life pilot testing reflected these statistics; most of the teachers did not have student computers in their classrooms. This came as something of a surprise, since the teachers in the first focus group were early adopters. Hence, the evaluators believed them to be those most likely to have computers, and they were. However, few of the applicants had enough or for that matter any computers in their classrooms beyond the computer on their desks. Nevertheless, the teachers without classroom computers were positive that they would be able to use computers in computer labs, another teacher's room, the library, or wherever they could find them. They also had naive assurances from their principals that they would provide teachers with the resources that were needed. There was no choice but to take everyone's word that this would work.

Electronic curriculum was the most expensive venture of all, and the path was not clear as it was with the first two technology stops. The central office and libraries followed the business route. Computers made what they were already doing easier and better. The goals of stakeholders were well defined. For example, states wanted to improve the quality, quantity, and rate of exchange of data. The results were easy to measure, and they could see them immediately. It was straightforward to justify initial funds and even easier to justify additional funds to maintain and even expand the data collection. The same with the library: technology increased the number of students using it. It also equalized information access, because even the poorest and remotest school could have access to databases and other information by using the Internet.

Electronic curriculum was unexplored territory, and, despite all the hype, money throwing, and parental expectations, no one was sure about the appropriate ways in which to use technology for teaching and learning. Does every student need a computer? Is it necessary to have every classroom emptied of desks and replaced with computers? Are teachers obsolete? Should schools build more labs and not put computers in the classroom? Should they expand libraries to be the main part of the school? The result was that stakeholders all contributed, but in small steps and small amounts, each experimenting with his or her idea of how electronic curriculum would be used in the classroom. This was a good thing.

At first, there was an expectation and optimism that the only thing schools had to do was get classrooms connected to the Internet. The materials and resources they needed would be there for free. This was a concrete start: wire classrooms so that students have access to computers. However, the expense of wiring a classroom, let alone twenty or thirty, was breathtaking. Not even all the stakeholders pooling their funds together could finance this venture. Nationally, the average age of school facilities was over forty years. The design of traditional classrooms does not allow for thirty computers, thirty desks, and space for students to move around. Also missing were the number of electrical outlets needed to power up all the computers and auxiliary equipment, access to the Internet, and ventilation for sixty hot bodies—half of those students, the other half computers. It looked as if schools needed to be remodeled and new schools built in order for classrooms to accommodate technology. But that didn't help early adopters, who had to experiment with different ways in which to use old rooms and new technology.

The value of the pilot testing is that it showed the vast variety of ways in which teachers could use technology. Sounds easy, but it was not. To acquire their computers, teachers had to be creative and resourceful. Most turned into grant writers, box-top-collecting entrepreneurs, or even dumpster divers. Then they took the motley collection of whatever they found, bought, or borrowed and assembled it into an effective learning environment. They also brought in a collection of auxiliary equipment like television sets, projectors, electronic whiteboards, handheld computers, and laptops. They matched the method of teaching to their circumstances depending on the number and types of equipment and the physical limitations of the room and school.

This period of experimentation was another stroke of luck that helped to advance technology integration because it compelled individual teachers to try out different types of electronic delivery in the classroom before any large purchases were made. The results have shown that there are many ways in which teachers can integrate technology by matching it with teaching strategy. Knowing this, business managers need to mediate in order to keep an open dialogue between staff and teachers on what the teaching goals are and the restrictions posed by facilities, equipment, and budgets. This can not only save money but also improve teaching and learning. The following are descriptions of how five teachers successfully used electronic delivery to solve the problems of bringing technology into their curricula.

One teacher found that the phone company, keen on cultivating future paid users, would provide free what was then high-speed access. She commandeered all the refurbished computers from the vocational education-technology classes. They had old and outdated Pentium III processors, but they had sufficient power to use the program. This was mainly because of the dedicated Internet connection—clear pipes meant a fast, stable connection that was not overcrowded by users from the rest of the school. She took all the desks out of the room, put in long rows of tables, and scattered the computers about. Her husband volunteered to string cable and electrical wires up to and over the ceiling, linking the computers to a dedicated Internet connection.

Televisions on tall stands were placed throughout the room with cables wandering along the floor hooking them up to the computer on her desk. These served as monitors for the students to see while she used the illustrations on her computer to highlight her lectures. The room was large and the screens were small, but numbers won in this case because all the students, leaning a bit this way or that, had a clear view of a television. The teacher's area was crowded with computers and printers of all types, including a dot matrix that was, even then, obsolete. With lab benches and sinks along two walls, the room also had facilities to be a wet lab for experiments.

The teacher usually began the lesson with a lecture demonstration. As she explained the process, she used the electronic activities to illustrate the concept. Even though there were many graphic choices, she used the overhead projector to show an illustration that she had always used before computers. After explaining the activity, the teacher asked the students to, on their own, read the textbook and then complete the online assignments. The textbook provided instructions to the students on what activities matched the reading, so the students could go back and forth from textbook to computer.

The students were accustomed to pushing and pulling the computers into various positions according to the activity they were doing. If it was a textbook activity, they pushed the computers to the side, stacking the keyboard and mouse on top of the monitor. If it was a computer activity, they arranged them in many different ways. More social students tilted the computers to connect to the people they were next to or across from. Less social students prudently aligned themselves directly in front of the screen, blocking out contact with others. While doing an activity, some students kept their books on their laps, religiously following the textbook directions. Others were flying all over the electronic activities, ignoring the textbooks as they interacted with their neighbors and talked.

This model is an important one for how a teacher can economically gather enough equipment to have a rich array of technology. It also was a model for how you don't need the biggest and greatest computers. She needed running computers for her classroom, other materials, supplemental Web sites, and PowerPoint demonstrations—simple needs that don't require lots of memory or speed. There was no need to network her computers with the rest of the school. She didn't need expensive licenses, application programs like word processing, or memory-gobbling programs to manipulate photographs or illustrations.

She was a model for getting outside help and using old, borrowed, and stolen equipment that she scrounged from the entire school seemed very resourceful. However, after a quick tour of other classrooms, it was noticed that most of the teachers from whom she had gotten the televisions did not replace them. She had an abundance of computers from the vocational classes, but she took most of them; other teachers did not have that resource. Her class was rich in technology, but others were not. This pattern was repeated in most schools. There was more of a technology gap between teachers in a school than there was between schools. For example, a student could be attending the most advanced high school in the state and still not have a class where the teacher uses technology. Technology use is teacher-dependent.

A teacher in another school had a room that was built for about ten fewer students than she had, not an uncommon situation. She arranged the computers in a single row on the science-lab benches that lined two sides of the room. The benches were high and built-in with traditional black slate tops, outlets for gas, and sinks for water. In the back of the room, the teacher created a makeshift bench by putting two tables together for the extra students. The lab stools for the high benches had long since been taken away to accommodate the extra desks tightly stuffed in the room. The students at the "bench" in the back of the room had no choice but to use chairs. The class period was long, so the teacher rotated the students so everyone had an equal opportunity to stand and to sit.

The computers, like the others described above, were a motley assemblage of brands, power, and monitors. The teacher was a successful grant writer, and there was an additional win with this. Because of her resourcefulness in acquiring outside money and using technology, the principal continually reinforced her achievements by supplying more technology. As the old equipment faded, he helped replace it, and if the grant did not quite cover all the equipment needed, he supplemented it. During an interview with him, he confirmed that the teachers in his school who used technology were rewarded with more technology when funds became available. This behavior and action turned out to be common among principals, system managers, and district people. Teachers who used technology got technology.

The teacher's ability to win grant money was largely attributed to her participation in professional organizations. She was an excellent model for how teachers could acquire equipment by networking at national, state, and local professional organizations. She was very active in the American Association of Biology Teachers, attended presented sessions regularly, and was an officer on the board of directors. She was one of the original teachers who participated in listservs for biology teachers. Locally, she was also active conducting workshops for her peers on how to use animals in the classroom and hands-on labs. Vendors, organizations, and administrators viewed her as a master teacher and invested money and time for her to share her knowledge with other teachers.

The next teacher described never managed to get computers in her classroom but was still able to provide a technology-rich learning experience. Remember the students stuck in the doorway temporarily stopping the flow of traffic? Despite the difficulty of using labs, the teacher was successful in making them a regular part of her routine by gaining the principal's support for priority scheduling. After she commandeered retired lab computers, she knew she was going to have to change her strategy for technology. She had Internet access at her desk, and she mistakenly thought that it would be easy to get the computers wired. She didn't have the resources of the free volunteer tech staff that the other teacher had. Staff would have had to wire the room and upgrade the computers. Money was an important factor that prevented this. Trying to get overworked technology staff scheduled to do the work was the other factor. They wouldn't have time until summer break.

However, she knew better than to rely on the lab alone and used a combination of resources to meet her teaching goals. Through networking and searching the Internet, she found a company that sold electronic whiteboards and negotiated free use of the equipment in exchange for writing articles about her experience. Electronic whiteboards were just beginning to be introduced to the education community, and manufacturers were looking for teacher endorsements. She also found a grade book and quizzing software package that had been developed by a regional university.

Electronic whiteboards become a computer monitor but are even better than a monitor is because the image can be written over. After a lecture using the graphics and interactives, the notes, arrows, diagrams, and highlights can all be saved to the teacher's computer, sent by e-mail, or printed out. The contrast of the professional presentation of the text and the teacher's scribbled, handwritten notes effectively draws the students' attention to specific concepts. An added software feature was that the students were connected at their desks. The teacher could present a situation and a couple of solutions, and the students could immediately respond with an answer. Their responses would be tabulated collectively as a vote for the right answer, but she could also see individual responses. The value to the students was that it kept them engaged in the lecture. The value to the teacher was that she could instantly evaluate how successful the lesson was and who understood the concepts and who did not. She could then immediately adjust her teaching to slow down or speed up or to wake up a student.

The teacher used the quizzing software as individual homework. The students were to answer a quiz, and it was pretty tough. After they took the quiz, the software reported how many questions the students answered correctly and how many they got wrong. They could take the quiz as many times as they wanted until they got all the answers correct. In order to do this, the students had to revisit every question and confirm their answers. The quiz would lock up when the homework was due, so it was a race for time to get all the questions correct. The exercise took on a gamelike quality when, in the computer lab, the students could work together to get all the answers.

Schools increasingly are bypassing cable to use wireless connections and purchase laptop computers. This added a new hope to the likelihood of using computers in a traditional lecture-style classroom. Unlike the desktop computers, laptops can be put on students' desks; hence, they do not demand additional space in already too-crowded rooms. Students had complete freedom to spread out and use the laptops wherever the action was—under the desk is a favorite spot in one classroom. Neither is it necessary to string cable around the classroom for an Internet connection or to put in more outlets to plug the computers in.

The most promising use of a traditional classroom observed was one that combined many different venues for technology that fit well within the restrictions of the room layout. The classroom had five desktop computers strung along a bench on one side of the room and five wireless laptops in a homemade Tupperware carrier. When students had computer assignments, they were able to create the type of personal atmosphere that suited their learning preferences. The students who gravitated toward the line of computers tended to be more social and ended up in loosely organized groups that expanded and shrank as students gravitated from one cluster to another. Other students took the laptops to their desks and quietly worked in pairs. Two students worked alone silently, one sitting on a lab bench, the other under it.

Wireless networks solved the problem of stringing expensive cables. However, an amusing precursor to the story is that half of the laptops were registered with one wireless hub, and the remainder were registered with another. This happened because the building was U-shaped. One hub was on one side of the U and the other on the other side of the U. The classroom was in the bottom center of the U, and both signals came into the classroom but with weak reception. Not knowing which computers were registered with which hub, the students carried the laptops around like divining rods until they could pick up a signal.

The teacher also acquired an electronic whiteboard and an oversized wireless keyboard and mouse that could be passed around between the students. When she was giving a lecture, she projected the activities onto the whiteboard with the students sitting at their desks in traditional classroom style. She would give one student the keyboard and ask him or her to operate the activity while she talked through the concept. She would then ask questions, calling on individuals to check their understanding. The students could also ask questions with the teacher using the illustrations or activities to explain. It was very much a lecture enhanced with visuals, activities, and student participation.

This teacher was a model for how an eclectic mix of technology can be employed to vary the types of teaching strategies, hence reaching students with varied learning preferences. As she acquired new types of technology, she used them to complement and improve the teaching strategies she was using. Lectures, once complemented with static overheads, were enhanced with interactive visuals and student interaction. Rather than completing worksheets, students could do activities that were interactive and respond to them individually at their own pace.

SUMMARY

Two lessons were learned here for business managers. One is that technology increased the effectiveness of support services. The central office and library can contribute to educating students. The increased data that the central office can collect and crunch with computers provides the statistical tools for analysis of the areas of excellence and areas that need more attention. The library is much better prepared to serve students and teachers with the expanded resources technology offers than it ever possibly could have imagined with paper resources.

Second, schools will always have restrictions and limitations due to the facilities. The teacher examples here showed how they could respond within the parameters of the facilities, but they also showed that the facilities are not gatekeepers to integration of technology. None of these descriptions was of a perfect classroom, but the classrooms were effective models to show the variety of ways in which teachers can adapt a traditional room to accommodate technology. The pattern that emerged was that all the teachers were able to create ways in which they could match technology and teaching style within the confines of the facilities the school provided.

It also showed a grave concern. Technology integration into the curriculum is too often dangerously teacher-dependent. A student can attend the most prestigious school in the state and have no opportunity to use electronic materials. However, this teacher dependence can be advantageous, because a student can attend the lowest-rated school in the state and have a classroom rich in technology and opportunities to use materials out of school as well. A solution to this is that the electronic materials that the school selects have to fit the facilities. Another is that business managers need to work to even out the playing field by coordinating technology infrastructure and budgets to ensure that all teachers have options and incentives to provide students with electronic opportunities.

Chapter Eight

Enter the Techies

Even with all the influence federal and state stakeholders have because of the money they give, they still only have partial control of individual schools' technology infrastructure. That also is a good thing. The schools and districts do have a great deal of academic freedom in how they may manage their own infrastructure. As processes and mechanics of technology stabilized, much has become regular routine; however, as we have seen, there are many ways in which technology can enter schools, and, once there, there are many more ways in which it can fit into the restrictions of facilities. How all this is managed is the responsibility of the business manager. As technology expanded and matured, tech staff members were added to support the teachers and support-services staff. Their task was to make technology work. To an outsider, watching all these personalities negotiate together can be amusing. For those business managers who have to manage and budget for the chaos, it can be daunting pandemonium.

In early years, it was found that even when individual teachers, staff members, or administrators acquired computers on their own, they could not sustain them alone and work independently without technical support and cooperation from the rest of the school. The facilities, technical, and management staff all have to play some part in keeping technology up and running throughout the school. Applause, applause to the people who go the extra mile to bring in technology. However, too many independent decisions with conflicting goals and objectives, even though well meant, can throw a school into uncontrolled emergencies and cause knee-jerk reactions, resulting in lots of money spent but very little accomplished. Free computers are very much like free kittens. The care and feeding is where one has to pay the price. The initial cost of the computer is a small percentage of the total cost of ownership (TCO).[1]

A humorous (because it happened to someone else) example is one teacher who received a grant to purchase classroom presentation equipment: a computer, LCD projector, and printer. The teacher, anxious to begin instructing with technology, leafed through some advertising literature and purchased, among other things, a ceiling-mounted projector complete with installation. Since it didn't seem to affect what was happening with the rest of the school, the purchase was made without input from the technology staff. The company's technicians came, installed the projector on the ceiling, and left. The teacher, blissful with anticipation, entered the room to see a beautifully mounted three-thousand-dollar projector with an electrical cord unceremoniously hanging down, plugged into nothing. There was no electrical outlet in the ceiling. Installation meant the company installed it in the ceiling. That's it. The school had to provide the electrical connection.

It was a painful situation for everyone, because the teacher had promised to provide the funder with results of the project: no results, no more money. The school facilities staff had to rescue the project and run electricity to the projector, a very costly endeavor because staff had to wire the room out of sequence from their well-laid-out cost-effective plan for rewiring the entire school. Other teachers who did not have funded projects were inconvenienced and completely unhappy; they had to wait. The errant teacher had written new lesson plans, all based on using the presentation equipment. He also had to wait, begrudgingly, for two months to begin the new teaching endeavor. It was very, very frustrating for all. As the use of technology grew, there were thousands of incidents like this. These incidents happen when teachers and technology staff don't communicate.

This is also an example of the importance of the business manager mediating with the teacher and technical staff before the grant is written. Had the teacher been in touch with the business manager and technical staff, everyone would have been saved the frustrating, expensive, and unwanted situation. The grant could have been written to cover the cost of wiring, the teacher could have switched rooms to one that was wired, another funder could have been found to fund the wiring of the room, or, to gain the equipment and reputation for using technology, the school could have bitten the bullet and completed the project the same way but without surprises.

---

1. The Consortium for School Networking (CoSN) partnered with Gartner Consultants, who branded and popularized formulas that industry could use to determine the total cost of ownership for technology and other www.classroomtco.org/gartner_intro.html.

Lucky for kittens, the parents, as they are feeding the cat, always believe the child will take care of it, and, with technology, the same scenario occurs as school staff look to the business manager to rescue them. It was probably a good thing that the reality of the cost and staff needed to bring technology to the classroom was ignored or only slowly realized. No administrator would have allowed a computer to be plugged in if he or she had realized that an entire new genre of technological and managerial professionals would have to be hired and supported. In the beginning, it was fun for schools to write a play, make costumes, and save the farm, but that could not continue. Computers follow the simple principal law of life: what can go wrong will. Soon, the early adopters were overwhelmed.

The grassroots management approach that early adopters used for technical support was abruptly on its way out. Early adopters relied on their own initiative to maintain the computers and the Internet connections. They pretty much took care of themselves, even if their talent was in cajoling the administration for extra funds. But it was quickly getting out of hand. Twenty years ago, the teenage kid down the street could fix a car with a screwdriver and the contents of the silverware drawer. Computers were going the same way as cars. As long as the computer system in a school consisted of one or two teachers collecting a motley assemblage of technology and spending their free time fiddling with it to keep it going, it was manageable for the business manager. These teachers were like teenagers with 1957 Chevys.

It was interesting to watch the early adopters solve maintenance problems. One simply created a graveyard of misbehaving computers that teetered in a tower in the back of her room. As she acquired and used more computers, she systematically threw spent or annoying computers to their gymnastic fate where they would hopefully balance at the top of the pile. Some were really dead, but others just went out of date because they didn't have the power or capability to handle new rapid-fire, gamelike software, plug-ins, or Internet services. Some of them she just didn't know what to do with. Fortunately for her and the students, she was able to write and win grants faster than the students could go through computers. Not quite an efficient process of maintenance, but it worked for her. However, that was not a solution for the school.

At the same time that schools were being pressured to figure out how to maintain and manage computer infrastructure, the dot-com boom, with inflated salaries and promises of great stock options, lured every person who had a hint of technology talent or ability. Schools, not being prepared to pay such high salaries and not having the promise of stock options, were left to their own creative devices to find people to operate the systems. Generally, the first wave of technical staff was made up of teachers who *liked* computers. Liking computers meant that the teachers really thought computers were cool and would hopefully have the energy and interest to learn what was needed to maintain them, mostly on their own time. The common way to reimburse the teachers-turned-techies was to give them release time. Instead of teaching five classes, they would teach three, which freed up some hours of the day for working with the computers and other teachers.

Their support and supervision was often the principal crossing his or her fingers that the teachers could magically keep up with technology and the ever-increasing number of computers. Without work models, job descriptions, or experience to draw on, the quality and quantity of work varied with the individual personality, initiative, and work ethic. The degree of commitment and production varied greatly from school to school. One school had a philosopher who wrote copious volumes on the theoretical uses of computers. Another school had someone who loved to tinker with the inner workings of each computer, adding parts here and there to make the computer go faster or accommodate different operating systems. The most extreme example was one school that had a teacher who could no longer handle the classroom and was sent to the computer lab to keep the computers running and monitor the students' Internet use. Rather than fixing computers, she spent her time running from computer to computer as the students teased her by making illegal Web sites appear and disappear the closer she came. But thankfully, most schools had individuals who were capable and willing, albeit untrained, to do the job.

For early adopters—teachers who liked technology—there was little technical, financial, or administrative support beyond the principal-turned-faith healer. As computer systems became more complex and grander, retaining teachers in part-time tech positions proved to be expensive and only marginally effective. When a teacher needed help in his or her classroom, it was seldom at the same time as the two or three hours of release time that the tech teacher received each day in exchange for maintenance. Plus the working hours for which tech teachers were paid were monopolized with fixing computers, not professional development to keep up with new technologies. If they did keep up, it was during their own time and at their own initiative. Pondering the structure of the technology infrastructure and architecture was a luxury set aside in favor of survival.

The next genre of computer support services that technologists observed were recruited via the "raise your own" method of recruitment. Trusted students who liked computers were added as additional support staff, sometimes working between classes or after school. Some of them had more experience messing around with computers than the teachers-turned-techs who supervised them. These students often become long-term employees, remaining with the school after graduation from high school or coming back after earning postsecondary technical degrees. They have a sense of history that is important to stability but often not for innovation.

Outside pressure from educators, parents, and legislators to purchase computers and Internet access weighed heavily on the schools, but for those applying pressure, there was much less hoopla about how technology would be maintained once there. Meanwhile, more and more computers began arriving to the schools with no one to install them, plug them in, and keep them running. Part-time and unskilled maintenance threatened the stability and peace of the school. In the midst of all the screams and the pending anarchy from overstressed technology-using teachers and abused technology staff, schools, feeling like they were being hit with a baseball between the eyes, began to realize that they needed to hire professional technical staff to bring some type of order to an increasingly messy system.

Thankfully, the dot-com bust made stable, steady jobs at schools look good to the wounded soldiers emerging from the rubble. When professional staff walked into a school, they were greeted with miles of wires and cables, heaps of computers, an astounding number of power strips, and naive but lovable teachers. Professional staff inherited an often ill-conceived technology infrastructure that grew like cancer. It was amazing to observe how individual schools solved the problems of connecting and plugging in. What was more amazing was that fire and safety measures were often overlooked by state inspectors and risk management staff, something that should make business managers cringe. There were so many weekend handyman tactics employed that one must semiseriously question whether the growth in the supermarket-style home improvement stores was due to schools purchasing supplies to string cable and run wires.

As the second wave of teachers, the early majority, began to use the computers, they put more and more pressure on the schools to learn how to manage all of this. The massive and growing number of student users; their constant, daylong, enthusiastic pounding; and the well-meaning but amateurish maintenance from teachers soon paralyzed the schools' ability to keep up with computer maintenance. Plus, there was a need to get serious about bringing computers to the classroom. Schools responded to all this by creating new positions: systems manager and technical-support staff. The new technology staff came from a different culture: business. This instantly enlivened school politics as the thrones of the early adopters were challenged and layers of authority were added. The early adopters, used to having complete and absolute control and power over their computers, began to lose it to the newly hired techies. They were used to doing what they wanted, when they wanted, how they wanted. Suddenly technology decisions had to be made according to what was best for the school, not the individual teacher. Ouch! Battle lines were drawn as two cultures clashed. This is a continuing situation that business managers will have to mediate and solve.

New tech staff also had to address the often neglected or ignored issue of not having sufficient electricity to plug everything in. What they saw when they walked into a room was a scene similar to what most have experienced when decorating for Christmas. At some point, the tree lights, angels, candles, trains, Santa's village, and sparkling reindeer all have to be plugged in. It is one of those bewilderingly head-scratching activities people ponder and deliberate over as they hold twelve plugs and look at one socket. It was not unusual for classrooms in even not-so-old buildings to only have one or two outlets. Biology and other science rooms fared better than most because even some of the older schools had outlets for students to plug in microscopes. If a lab area was attached, then they often had enough outlets for computers at the lab benches. However, for most classrooms, like most homes, the solution was power strips, lots and lots of power strips, and eggnog, lots and lots of eggnog.

In most traditional classrooms observed, the room was full of makeshift barriers constructed to keep the cables and wires out of harm's way so as not to trip students. This was mostly unsuccessful for the observers who, unaware of the hazards, spent most of the time stumbling over wires and cable. It was surprising not to see orange traffic cones. The students became artful dodgers to avoid getting tangled up while still exchanging pleasantries, gossip, and jabs. Plugging in computers meant using extension cords, power strips, and plastic molding; apparatus to hold wires, hooks, and PVC pipe; and plastic mats to jury-rig outlets.

The introduction of laptops rescued some schools from having to rewire rooms; students could use them without plugging them in. This appeared to be a simple solution to the problem of not enough outlets, and it would have been except for the batteries. Batteries solved the electric problem but created another problem. Most classroom sets of laptops come with a rolling cart with bays for each computer to be plugged into the cart. Then the whole cart is plugged into the one wall socket. However, batteries had enough juice for three or four class periods. By the end of the third class, the computers died. It took almost as much time to charge up a computer as it did to use it. Even if the students plugged them back into their bays, the recharging time between classes was not sufficient to energize the batteries.

The next problem that was witnessed was that by the end of the year was that many of the batteries were beginning to fade. By the second year, the batteries began needing replacement. One school had exhausted their technology budget, and the cost of the batteries was an expenditure no one had put into the budget. As the batteries died one by one, they had to resort to plugging in the laptops and were back to the outlet problem. This is very typical of challenges in technology: solve one setback only to discover another.

Security was another issue that was getting out of hand. The most interesting pornography avoidance plan was the Mabel plan. During a workshop to train early adopters to use computers, two teachers had teamed up, each with their own computer separated by a panel. One was always one click ahead of the other. As the instructor guided them from one site to the next, both friends would make the click. Mabel would click and then quickly shut her eyes, sitting motionless. Her friend would scrutinize the new site, pop up over the panel and say, "Okay, you can look now." Mabel's shoulders would relax, and she would bend over to confidently look at the site. What were they doing? Mabel's friend was alerting her if the new site might contain pornography. Interesting system, but it is not quite practical for general application. Mabel and her friend are probably one of a kind.

As schools began to do the numbers on the cost of maintaining technology, they found that they were spending far less for computers and infrastructure than businesses did; it was about half of what business spent. This probably could be attributed to schools being flooded with energized amateurs, volunteers, teachers, parents, local businesses, and spouses. They did what industry never could do—find people to work for little to no riches or even promises of riches. Looking at the amount of dollars spent for the amount of progress made, this volunteer army was impressive. Schools showed that energy and volunteers have an important role in making things happen, but they don't eliminate pain. The well-meaning volunteer efforts sometimes cost more than if the job had been done professionally. The quality and quantity of service, products, and support bounced up and down depending on the person leading and the synergy of the volunteers.

SUMMARY

As professional technical staff began taking their positions, it was obvious that there was no pattern or consistency in how schools started the foundation of their technology infrastructure. Although schools all faced the same challenge—providing computer maintenance and Internet service to hundreds of computers and other electronic equipment—schools were all attacking it differently according to the facilities, budgets, and wiring issues and the plunder of early adopters. The one thing they had in common was that they needed to find some way to govern and manage technology and bring the chaos under control, because the job of providing technology to all areas of the school was much more complex than imagined. Volunteers could not be abandoned, but they could not do it alone. In order to accomplish this, the business manager needs to exhibit strong leadership so he or she can mediate between technology staff, teachers, and support staff.

Chapter Nine

Managing Chaos

What most teachers wanted, or thought they wanted, was a computer repair-person. What they got, if they were lucky, was another team member to work with the business manager to govern and manage the technological infra-structure of the school. Governing technology means strategic planning be-yond what is happening every day in isolated classrooms, being a team member in planning for the future technology needs of the entire school. The job is much more complex than just installing and fixing computers. It in-cludes designing the infrastructure of the computers that are networked; making decisions on what hardware and software to purchase, when to up-grade, what auxiliary equipment to purchase; and keeping up with innova-tion. It is a huge management task, and it is impossible without governance to build guidelines to direct the school on the path that addresses the needs of its particular learners.

All the computers in the school contribute toward a better learning envi-ronment. The challenge is to network them so they can seamlessly communi-cate with each other. Systems managers and technology staff are responsible for building and then implementing computer networks, both intranet net-works, which link the school's computers together, and Internet networks, which link all computers to the world. Computers have to have software in-stalled, ranging from the school's ultrasecure database to various teaching software by levels and disciplines and even a computer that operates the heat-ing system. Then computers have to be continually updated. This will never change. Upgrades also have to be made to the hardware through the installa-tion of additional memory, video cards, hard drives, monitors, CD drives, and so on. School facilities need to be upgraded. Over 40 percent of the schools in the United States are in inadequate buildings, but, in disrepair or not, they are all charged with upgrading electrical wiring and weaving cable from computer to computer and then out to the Internet.

Tech staff by default inherited an infrastructure in which they had to be experts in every type of technology, since teachers, support staff, and administrators had gone to the pound and adopted kittens, puppies, snakes, and even a raccoon. Teachers, staff, and administrators weren't programmed to consider how their equipment would factor into maintaining the entire collection of the school, but tech staff had to. For example, there was a teacher who had scrambled together a vast collection of old and new technology. She was considering a move to another school. When she left, she planned for her entire rich technology infrastructure to go with her.

But the story gets more interesting. When the systems manager of her school was interviewed about how they managed technology, she relayed that they were trying to establish some order in the chaos. No technology could be purchased without the consent of the systems manager. No brands and models beyond the two approved by the technology committee. No used computers, no hybrids, and no computers with operating systems less than Windows 2000. No Macs. No processors less than a Pentium III. No hard drives less than three gigabytes. There was a large list of noes, all of which described the teacher's classroom.

When the principal was interviewed, the interviewer asked how the teacher's classroom was able to operate under such strict rules that clearly defined the room as illegal. The principal just sighed and said, "Everyone ignores that room." Administration and tech staff silently acknowledged that the teacher affected well over a hundred students each year with a technology-rich curriculum, and the school's financial and staff-time investment was minimal. No one was going to go in and tell the teacher she could not have her computers and take that away from the students. A room that was tech-support-free was the anomaly, not the norm. However, a battle was brewing over whether the teacher could move all her equipment with her. It brewed on many levels: the teacher wanted to take the equipment, the school wanted to keep the resources, and the technology people feared what might be needed to keep the room going without volunteer help.

Business managers will constantly be faced with the situation of making judgments about controls. This is a part of governance. At a technology conference, a group of systems managers were overheard discussing the idea that no teachers, or anyone for that matter, should be allowed to bring in technology without the specific okay from them. This is as dangerous a situation as allowing anything to be brought in on a whim. Controls that are too tight can paralyze a system by eliminating the ability to respond to unexpected opportunities—the essence of how educational innovation is funded and takes hold.

Encouragement of individual actions by early adopters or visionary administrators was built into the system of schools—whether accidentally or intentionally, no one knows for sure. Innovators need to have the freedom and encouragement to grab onto windfall opportunities that pop up from government, industry, or the sky. Had there been overly strict controls, technology would not have had the experimental period necessary to discovering its role in teaching and support.

Business managers will have to work with tech staff to determine how money can be spent and who will be allowed to make purchases. This also is part of governance. Developers with glitzy, massive, and well-brochured sales forces are keenly aware of the deep pockets among the multiple stakeholders. After golf games at the club, conferences, or sales visits, tech staff, sitting in their offices, would find themselves surprised with a new program, computers, or equipment. Schools have to judge whether a product is indeed good or whether its best feature is its sales force.

One observed school had the most up-to-date science equipment for hands-on labs stuffed in old-style classrooms. They had incubators, centrifuges, microscopes, a crazy mirror reflecting the teachers' demonstration table in the front of the room, a flame hood, a mini-greenhouse, and a refrigerator spread out among three rooms. All this sounded really great until the students tried to do an experiment. The desks had to be shoved together to the side to be out of the way of equipment doors when they were swung open. Some equipment had to be rolled out into the room to be used. Sometimes students had to go from room to room to complete one experiment since the equipment had been installed by size, not by use. The administrator, basking in the glow of creating an innovative technological school, moved on to greener pastures, leaving the teachers and tech staff pondering what to do.

Having both short- and long-term plans for technology in which everyone has input sets down guidelines for purchasing that can focus stakeholders when they do have money to spend. This provides everyone with a plan for what purchases will be the most useful to the schools. These recommendations assist stakeholders in knowing what should be done to be in alignment with the goals and objectives of the school. Rather than stakeholders making decisions by guessing or with the help of a salesperson, they can use the school's governance plan to wisely determine what they need to purchase to fulfill the true needs of the school.

Technology staff can also help business managers decide what operating system, or perhaps even multiple systems, is (are) the best for the school. The operating system is what marries the software with the computer applications. If a piece of software is not compatible with the operating system, nothing will happen. The plug-ins, the Web-enhancement software that makes things move, jump, and rotate for programs, require certain editions of an operating system and vice versa. Therefore, frustratingly, some things are compatible with some things some of the time but not anything all of the time.

The effects of this were very apparent during testing of products. Netscape and Internet Explorer were trying to elbow each other out. Microsoft went into full battle. At first, one program only worked best on Internet Explorer, but not all schools had Internet Explorer. It seems simple to download a browser, but it is not if it has to be done on hundreds of computers quickly. In order for the small tech staff to control the software and upgrades, they created an intranet that networked all the computers in the school. They could sit in their offices, push the software out to all the computers, and, at the same time, wipe out all the illegal downloads the students, teachers, and staff made during the day.

The day before a teacher was to pilot test a unit, she had a tech-staff person download the required browser and plug-ins to the lab computers. However, a well-organized and dutiful tech person pushed the computers that night, wiping out the new downloads and reinstalling the old software. The tech person used a disk that had the optimal software for all the programs that were currently running. They had an older version of Internet Explorer, but it was the perfect formula for the school's software. Everything worked fine until the new edition curriculum was added. Then the fun began. The new program would not run on the old software. The teacher, thinking that she had the right edition, could not get the interactives to work. Thinking she had everything right, she blamed the program for not working.

In another test, a teacher and a tech person had to endure the wrath of a colleague who could not get her software to work because the tech person had installed upgrades to the operating system—not a pretty scene. An upgrade is not an independent action. A computer's processor, operating system, memory, hard-drive space, or other software put restrictions on what can be upgraded and what cannot. For example, a computer could have the right operating system to match a new software program but not have a processor that is fast enough or has enough memory to run it. An Internet-based program could only be compatible with one browser and not another. Or the videos on a Web site may use two or three different types of video players, all of which are incompatible with the browser. It is like solving a Rubik's Cube.

It costs a great deal in money and staff time to upgrade plug-ins or browsers, and each time, especially when upgrading operating systems, upgrades can cause the dominoes to fall. That is because at some point all the software programs in the central office, library, and classrooms will have to be upgraded. It is sad, but there will be casualties. With some old programs, the company that produced them no longer exists, long swallowed up in a chain of acquisitions. Sometimes the sales of a program slump, and the company, no longer seeing a profit, discontinues it. Other times, the program has gone through so many new editions since it was purchased by the school that it can no longer be upgraded, but a new, whopping, more expensive edition is available.

To avoid this type of mismatched software, businesses adopted the practice of upgrading operating systems and getting rid of old computers about every three years or so. This is an effective course of action; however, schools cannot afford to do this. Because of the high cost of a new edition, the risk to older software, and the amount of staff time it takes to upgrade it, schools can only upgrade the operating systems every five to seven years. This strategy was also blindsided by stakeholders. Because of the pressure from stakeholders for schools to provide all students with technology-rich learning, schools cannot retire the old computers even if they upgrade operating systems. They need numbers. As long as a computer keeps running, even limping, with the screen green, the *n*-key not working, and continual crashing, it stays. But this means that a school could have one hundred computers consisting of a bunch of Macs and another bunch of PCs, all with different operating systems, speed, and memory. It is a talented and persistent tech person who can find a formula to accommodate the multitude of brands of software programs and hardware in a school.

Business managers and tech staff will constantly have to deal with this mismatch on two levels. One level is working with teachers and staff to decide the time line of when systems will be upgraded and work with teachers to decide what will be salvaged and what will be replaced. The other is working with companies who make software and operating systems to guarantee some type of stability over time. A new purchase is warranted because there is a vast improvement in what a program does, not simply because it was knocked out of the saddle by a new operating system.

Compatibility issues occur in other areas besides the computers and software. Internet connections are also a challenge. In one school being observed, the minute the bell rang all of the teachers, office workers, and students in computer labs, classrooms, and the library sat down to their computers and simultaneously logged on to the computers and then the Internet. Nothing happened. Amid the quiet, yeah's could be heard as one computer at a time managed to get a connection. In another instance, all the students hitting the computers at one time caused a bottleneck. Remember the students jammed in the doorway as they tried to get in and out of the lab? Well, the Internet does that too. A school full of computers all demanding to get on the Internet results in a bottleneck. Some currents get stuck in the doorway, stopping or at least slowing down the flow as they untangle themselves and get in line, single file, waiting to go through the narrow pathway.

The actual class-work time in this example was lessened by almost five minutes just because of getting the students logged on. Add that to the first five minutes it requires for students to rev up, and it is a serious concern because it takes time away from lessons. It doesn't sound like much time, but it is. Five minutes of class time is precious. It can mean the difference between doing and not doing an interactive or hands-on lesson, having time for the students to ask questions, or having time for the teacher to use questions to check student learning. The teacher having time to walk around and work with students individually makes a difference. The disruption also sets students off. They have a harder time settling down to business when they spend so much time clicking and waiting.

The reason this school had problems was lack of compatibility with the outside Internet connection. Think of the information flowing in and out of a school as a flow of water. The larger the pipe, the greater the amount of water that can flow, but if a large pipe connects to a smaller pipe, the flow of water slows down. In this case, the brand new pipes inside and around the school connecting all the computers were large, allowing lots of information to flow from one computer to the next. However, the older pipes leading into the school were much smaller. Or, think of it like a four-lane highway under construction where the workers close all but one lane. Traffic will come to a standstill as the cars wait for their turns to run the obstacle course of pylons.

In other instances, computers were slowed because students had to log on to the school's intranet before they could get on the Internet. The schools used this to track students but also to ensure that the users were qualified or cleared to use the computers. It was the same thing as with the Internet but much worse. The schools' computers were not able to handle the traffic of students, teachers, and support staff all simultaneously logging in. The schools had difficulty financing the fastest equipment to meet the demands of hundreds of computers firing up at 8:15 a.m., five minutes after the opening bell rang.

This is another part of governance and of management. Just as the computers in a school are not independent from another, the school is not independent from the district or Internet provider. As the school needs change, the outside world must change with them to provide them with access. Schools need to project the computing power they will need so that providers can also plan how they are going to boost their services and plan their workday. If a school has a governance plan, this helps providers to plan how they might fit into the needs of the school, in the same way that it guides stakeholders.

Another complication came when the filtering software required by another stakeholder, the federal government, was mandated. The intention was to prevent students from getting on sexually explicit Web pages. It didn't, but it did dramatically slow the process of students logging on. Filters are interesting animals. Filters should have prevented a person from logging on to an e-mail account or a pornographic site. This wasn't true. During observations, it was easy for observers to check their e-mail. But filters do add a time delay while logging on and frustration while using the computer. Both of these elements added to the teachers' exasperation with using technology and interfered with systems managers' ability to get fast, well-organized access for students.

Filters were devised at a time when it was thought that students would wander around the Internet in search of knowledge from sites produced by scientists, mathematicians, educators and the like. Few considered the idea that pornography and other equally objectionable sites would exist. When this was realized, generic filters became prophylactics that would detect sites that were unsuitable for students. Not to credit the pornography industry with any type of computer intelligence, the school's filters are easy to beat, not even close to stopping them from popping up. What the industry can't get past, the students can. However, pornography is not the only objectionable thing on the Internet. Students can get on sites that give them information about the current antics of the celebrity du jour, fashion, movie schedules, public gatherings, and other delightful but not-for-school-time sites.

Part of governance is business and technology staff working with support staff and teachers to figure out how they are going to use the Internet without the burden of filters or the time-wasting activity of constantly policing students. Schools may use the power of banding together to demand better filters or commercial products that guide students rather than restrict them.

The above examples are not different from what industry was experiencing in building a technology infrastructure to meet the needs of the company and the clients, but schools were doing it without the funds. Those business folks reading this will be objecting. Few enterprises have an overabundance of dollars with which to do things right. Schools only had the funds to do things wrong but had to find a way to do things right. Since professional technology-staff members have been hired, they have been playing catch-up. Now the time has come for technology staff to be more involved with planning and management rather than absorbed with crisis management.

Part of governance for business managers is making sure that technical staff have the professional-development opportunities to keep them informed of what other schools are doing, what works, and what is coming down the pike. Professional organizations are a key way for school technology staff to continually keep up with innovation, change, and improvements. At conference after conference it was enlightening to witness tech staff interacting with peers and connecting with others experiencing similar challenges. The solutions to building infrastructure were hashed out at conferences and in e-mail exchanges after everyone went home. Electronic communications are important for connecting technology staff. The innovation will still need to happen, because the schools have sufficient infrastructure to really begin the next level, which is to truly integrate technology with students in the classroom.

SUMMARY

Electronic curriculum will push the system for tech staff much more than will teachers occasionally grabbing lessons over the Internet. It is going to be tough. Electronic curriculum will be used daily and will be so integrated with other curriculum that it will demand much more stability and reliability of computers, Internet connectivity, and physical space. This next step will also require that schools rein in industry to produce products that meet the qualifications and limitations of the facilities and budgets under which schools must operate. Schools do have the buying power to do that. Up until now, they have not had the technology infrastructure to do anything more than flirt with producers of materials. To do this, schools will need to have some standards for the types of infrastructure they will have and will need to set goals for what standards material developers will have to meet.

Chapter Ten

What Business Managers Need to Know from Technical Staff

Teachers and support staff are more comfortable using computers and are beginning to think of them as a commodity, something they need in order to complete everyday tasks. Teachers turn on their computers like turning on their lights. Technology staff members are settling into their jobs, creating their job descriptions, and defining tasks as new situations come up. The situation that schools find themselves in is that technology staffers, once busy with the physical aspects of getting technology around the school, are needed in a different role than when they first came on board. That new role is to focus on supporting classroom teachers as they begin integrating technology into the curriculum. This will entail working with teachers, support staff, and material developers to fine-tune what support services can do. Simply, technicians will ask teachers what they need to do and then find ways technology can do it.

An effective technology infrastructure balances on the degree of talent, dedication, and knowledge of the technology staff and how well prepared they are for the job. There are many different areas of higher education from which technology staff can be hired. They can have a technological systems administration or computer degree earned from a four-year college or an applied science technical degree from a one- or two-year program. The advantage is that candidates have a heavy technological background with a firm foundation in systems management and maintenance. The disadvantage is that they will have little training in using technology for teaching and come from a different culture than educators. A certain amount of acculturation will have to occur, and much of that will be on the shoulders of the business manager.

Another area in higher education from which technology staff can come is an instructional design program in a four-year college or, less commonly, a two-year applied program. Instructional designers have training in creating learning programs. Depending on where they do their training and under whom they train, they may have varying degrees of technical or educational expertise. If they come through an educational program, they could be heavy on pedagogy, applying learning theory to the design or the program. Or they might come from a more technical program and be more skilled in programming and navigational design. Their portfolios will show their expertise.

There isn't a set formula for the background technology staff need. It is pretty much determined by the individual needs and talent in the school. The first factor is the type of support the school receives from the district. If the district governs, operates, and manages the computer and network infrastructure, then the school can hire staff that are trained to help the teachers develop lessons and curricula and be perhaps less reliant on staff having the technical expertise to design the architecture for a network. If there is little technical support from the system or the school is large and requires highly technical staff, then it may behoove the school to hire someone whose first priority is technology. For the lucky schools that can hire more than one staff person, a mix of technical and instructional design people may be the best.

Together, business managers and technical staff must identify which of the school's technology needs are consistent and standard and which elements must be flexible and responsive to individual teaching techniques and support services. For example, central office technology for what and how data is collected must be consistent from one year to the next or compatible with new software or technology in order to be used comparatively. It must be standard, standard, standard. However, teachers will use technology differently from room to room and require different types of computing power and support among grades, disciplines, or even individual teachers. Hence, support and facilities for them must be more flexible in terms of what technologies might be used, where they will be used, how often, and the types of software and programs that they can run.

The path to technology has reversed. Early on, the path was to bring technology to the classroom and then learn what the teachers would do with it. Now, teachers tell technical staff what learning objectives they have and what programs they want to use. Technology staff members then find a way to make it happen. Although teachers and support staff have some educational background in technology, they rely on the expertise of technical staff as to which technology would be the best. For example, a teacher may know that he wants to generate tests that are graded electronically so that he can check on students' progress more often but may not know how to find the appropriate software or how to use it. Another teacher may want to purchase software so that students can compile portfolios of what they have learned. Both teachers may be unaware that one software program purchased for the entire school would provide the tools they both need and be available to other teachers as well. Technical staff also has the bigger picture of what would benefit the entire school, not just one classroom.

The tech staff is responsible for the entire school's technology infrastructure, which is the total design of the support system that manage all the technology hardware (computers, printers, LCD projectors, and so on), support and data-collecting software, and networks, both Internet and intranet. The infrastructure can be very complicated, and the technology staff must have the expertise to take the lead in managing support staff and to advise administration on the best ways to meld all the components together. The technology staff works with the administration, teachers, and staff in strategic planning for governing technology. They, in turn, manage the technology within the parameters that are defined.

The technology staff sets up the network, the way in which computers are connected together. It can be a very tangled web. All of the computers that are on the Internet are linked together to access the main connection to the Internet. Think of it like all the electric sockets in a house, which are connected to the one main line from the electric company coming into the house. In addition or in lieu of this connection, many schools also have an intranet, a restricted in-house network that connects computers. The intranet houses databases, e-mail, discussion groups, notices, and other services specific to the school, like student test information and individual demographic information. Another reason for the intranet is for tech staff to be able to control the computers for maintenance. Some schools have extranets, expanded intranets that parents, district, state, and other outside authorized users can access securely.

The technical staff is responsible for setting up the networking system according to the programs and curriculum the school is using. Not all computers have to be connected to the Internet or have unrestricted access. Tech staff can advise on what gets connected and what does not. For example, if the class is using software from a CD or software that is installed in a designated computer that has a specific use or purpose, it may not affect the rest of the school, or licensing may not be connected to the rest of the school's computers. The software may be limited to an operating system, and the technology staff won't have to upgrade the computer.

Some computers may be connected to the Internet but have restricted Internet access. For example, it is hard to imagine that first or second graders would be allowed to wander aimlessly and naively on the Internet. They may access a reading program on the Internet but have a filter installed to keep them on that one spot. Computers in places like the library where students do need the Internet for research may have less restricted access to the Internet.

These computers may also need to be linked in order for tech staff to upgrade and maintain the software.

Providing input for the appropriate physical environment for the technology, including lighting, acoustics, climate control, space, electrical connections, and security, will also be part of technical staff's jobs. The environment that the tech staff feels is efficient and affordable may conflict with the learning environment that the teachers want to create. For example, for technical staff, it may be as terrorizing as the scraping of fingernails across a blackboard to put computers on science-lab benches close to water, chemicals, and multitasking students. However, this learning environment is ideal for science classes. Sometimes the place teachers and tech staff agree is the best place for computers cannot be accommodated by the facilities staff. Matching environments and physical space is an area in which business managers should mediate. Martinis help.

Technology staff also provide training for general technology skills and integration of technology within the curriculum. This can be become delicate, because it is necessary to blend the technical as well as the pedagogic aspects of technology. For example, teachers may need training on how to use electronic classroom-management software to create tests, use discussion boards, or calculate the weights of grades between homework, tests, final exams, and projects. To optimize learning, teachers must have the expertise to match the technical skills they have mastered. It is not uncommon to have two training teams, one for technological skills, the other for designing electronic curriculum that teaches.

The next set of responsibilities is maintenance and technical support of technology. This is where teachers and front-office staff always sting technology staff. Servicing hundreds of computers is not an easy task; it is an impossible task. It has to be done, but it won't ever be done. Hands-on museums have a similar challenge to that of schools with hundreds of enthusiastic learners banging away on electronic equipment. The goal of most exhibit staff is to keep the hundreds of the exhibits working; however, even at the most well-maintained museum, it is a given that about 15 percent of the hands-on exhibits will be down at any time. The most common task is keeping up with repairing errant hardware: broken keys, mouses that don't function, screens that don't light up, systems crashes, printers that jam, LCD projector bulbs that burn out, screens that rip. . . . What can go wrong will. Maintenance does not just include the equipment in the classroom, library, labs and front office but also the servers and other computers in the back rooms that run the system.

Museum technical staff would love to have the same schedule as schools, with holidays and summers almost devoid of users. Schools are fortunate that their technical staffers have downtime away from teachers and students in order to work uninterrupted. When classes are in session, just keeping up with maintaining computers is usually the main task and hope for technical staff. This requires prioritizing maintenance schedules, creating a paperwork system for work orders, and scheduling technical staff. It can be expected that any computer could be down and that there will be a lag time for getting each computer fixed. Business managers often have to mediate between teachers and staff who all believe their computers take priority over others. During breaks and summer, tech staff can do installations or the types of tasks for which they need to be in front of computers.

Networking reappears in the maintenance category because technical staff has another reason for linking computers, and that is maintenance. Through the network, tech staff has access to the hard drives and desktops of all computers from the safety of their offices. Upgrades, installing programs, reimaging, and other maintenance tasks can be accomplished without tech staff leaving their offices. Travel time is expensive and time-consuming. The more that can be accomplished from a central location, the better. That also raises conflicts related to standardizing computers and losing old or new software. Tech staff want access to computers for uniformity, and teachers want it for uniqueness.

Infrastructure also includes dealing with contracts, consultants, and vendors to obtain the needed technologies and software. The market is highly competitive and will be more so as more software companies and publishers gear up to design and build better programs for teaching. The increase in educational products produced commercially will intensify as students gain daily and reliable access to computers. This will require technology staff to act as futurists and guide wisely as teachers, staff, and administrators are influenced by the army of glitzy hardware and software salespeople that flood each layer of stakeholders. Technology staff need to be in the beginning loop in the consideration of new products' effectiveness and consideration of issues of installation and maintenance.

Business managers also need to involve technical staff in working with teachers to design fundraising strategies to attract gift-bearing stakeholders. Proposals are stronger if they show that the teachers have expert support and input from technical staff. If a teacher writes a grant for a room full of tablet PCs, the funder wants to know how they will be supported, if the school will have the applications and other software, and if the school will be able to pay licensing fees that the teachers say they will pay. Between writing a proposal and winning the competition, it can take up to a year before the school sees the money. It is not unusual to have to renegotiate grants to purchase up-to-date equipment or to ask for more money if the price has risen over the year since the grant was proposed.

Tech staff also need to keep abreast of innovations in hardware and judge if it is faddy, useful, or cost-effective for the learning potential. For example, iPods are making it easy and free for schools to put videos of lectures online. Students can download them for review 24/7 or as part of the class. In return for this free kitten, students need an iPod. Sounds frivolous at first, but iPods are less expensive than computers and easier and hardier for students to lug around. They solve many problems of absentee students missing lectures, help students who need more time digesting lectures, help tutors to better help students, and add to the flexibility of scheduling classes. However, to make videos of lectures requires video equipment, someone to operate the video, and training of teachers or staff. Business managers need to help teachers and tech staff weigh the cost, workload, and return when adopting new teaching technologies.

The operating system is what makes computers work. It will largely be the responsibility of the tech staff to determine which is best for the entire school and then to maintain it. The operating system interfaces between the software and hardware. The software tells the operating system what to do, and the operating system organizes the hardware to do it. Tech staff must be able to advise on what operating system is the best for the school to operate that day but must keep an eye on the future, because operating systems go out of date and then need to be upgraded. Every piece of software brought into the school must be evaluated for its ability to be compatible with the operating system.

Microsoft produces the most famous operating system, Apple the next. These are commercial products that are usually purchased along with the computer, but there is an alternative choice. Open-source operating system GNU/Lynx is fast growing in popularity. The best description of what open-source operating systems and software are comes from the GNU Web site. Think of open source as "free speech, not as free beer." It is, in a sense, free, but we are still talking kittens here. There is a cost to the operating system, but tech staff can adapt and alter the system without violating license agreements. This is a growing consideration. As more and more professional technology staff are hired, this may be a better option than more-restricted and less-flexible commercial systems.

In order for schools to be able to take advantage of the growing advantages of open source or other innovations, business managers need to be sure that technical staff are connected through professional organizations and publications. They need to connect and network through discussion groups, listservs, and other Internet sources where they can discuss successes and failures. As schools become more technology sophisticated and software is better defined as to what will be used and how often, open-source software may grow in popularity and even become the standard.

Applications are another area where tech staff will need to advise. These are standard, usually off-the-shelf, tools for basic tasks. The definitions of applications and software here are less complicated than in real practice. Applications include software for word processing, spreadsheets, and graphics programs that manipulate images and videos. Often, they are bundled in one suite like Microsoft Office or MacWorks. They are tools for everyday activities common to all students, teachers, and staff like word processing or spreadsheets.

Depending on the area and the use, tech staff have taken the lead in researching and advising on what applications the school will adopt. License fees have to be considered, because the cost of running similar but different brands of applications can be expensive. Some applications are more compatible than others are, and basic application programs may be standard, but the computers running them may not. Along with the applications and the types of computers, processing speed, operating system, and memory need to be considered. Matching computers with the correct amount of power can be very cost-effective. For example, the art classrooms would use drawing- and photograph-application programs requiring fast and powerful computers in order for students to do fine- and graphic-art pieces. The central office staff, which is producing newsletters, Web pages, and flyers, use word-processing and publishing applications that do not need high-end computers.

Software and programs are specially designed to do specific tasks that are usually independent from basic applications. Programs used in the classroom include learning or tutorial programs for reading, science, math, and phonics. They are specific for one academic level, interest, or grade. Although many programs were originally on CD, they are increasingly accessed online. This is where it becomes especially complicated for tech staff. Teachers, trained in teaching strategies, should take the lead in what types of software programs would match the teaching style and techniques they are using. Then tech staff need to match the programs with operating systems and equipment. They should be included in early discussions about what hardware should be purchased, the networking configuration, and what auxiliary hardware would be the most suitable for the budget and facilities and compatible with operating system and computers. They can also put the software purchase in perspective with all the other programs that are running in the school or district.

Advances in sound-editing, video-editing, and publishing software make it possible for technical staff to help teachers develop electronic curriculum that has the same professional look and quality of a commercial product, rather than looking like the handmade sweater Aunt Jane makes everyone for Christmas. This allows teachers and technical staff to collaborate to create grade-, academic-, geographic-, or discipline-specific software that complies with the core curriculum and standards of the school. Commercial software is developed for the largest number of users, like the large encyclopaedic-style textbooks that a school in inner-city New York can use as well as a school in rural Alabama. However, open-source software may be a way for individual schools to tailor a program to better suit the reading level and lessons and include geographic-specific information.

For example, the blue jay is prevalent in books and is common to the eastern part of the United States but is not common in the western part. An important learning tool for students is to use examples that are common to their everyday life so that the lesson is repeated and repeated every time they see the example. In southern Texas, they have a green jay. In California, they have a Steller's jay. Manipulatable and adaptable software could provide students with examples that are more representative of their areas. Areas where reading levels are low could alter the text to meet the reading level but still provide the material at the appropriate age or academic level.

The magic innovation was the CD, which could hold huge programs that could be downloaded to a computer or run on the side. A distinct advantage is that they do not require the Internet. This was an important factor as schools struggled to get sufficient access to serve classrooms. CDs were easily inserted into any computer, easily stored, and easy to copy. Teachers or students just pop them in, and they run. However, anything entrusted to the hands of a teacher or student is in peril of its life. There is no purposeful destruction, just the normal wear and tear of daily use.

Now that schools are getting reliable and fast Internet connections, programs that can be accessed over the Internet have distinct advantages both for the classroom and for maintenance. Students can't stomp on the Internet and break it, they can't get it stuck in a computer, and it is not reliant on teachers, students, and computers all being together at the same time. However, the Internet is not without planning, contemplation, and work for the tech staff. Wireless has helped because so many wires do not have to be connected, but one challenge meets another. In order for schools to take advantage of the improved delivery of content, it will be progressively more crucial for technical staff to build reliable Internet connections that teachers can add to their daily routine. Teachers will use the Internet dictated by curricula, not by when and if they can access the Internet.

Decisions that tech staff will need to discuss with teachers, staff, and administrators include how Internet access, the number of computers, and the environment will be matched with the curriculum. For example, should some disciplines or grades have labs with designated computer labs, workstations in each room, or thirty computers for at-will access? Filters need to be installed, but decisions will need to be made if they are to allow students unrestricted access to the Internet (except for the government-required restrictions on pornographic sites), limited access to targeted sites, or access to one site only.

Electronic classroom management portals are important tools for teachers. These are Internet or intranet portals that organize the daily lessons of a complete curriculum. They are most commonly used for distance education but are increasingly becoming popular for regular classrooms. They allow the teacher to collect and organize materials for daily lessons that students can access at school or even after school hours wherever they can find a connection. The materials teachers can include are readings, interactives, and materials they have produced or commercial activities. Portals also have chat rooms, message sending, e-mail, and other communication tools. Tests and multiple-choice, short-answer, or essay questions can be put online. Students can also post materials for projects, which can be included in their portfolios.

Grades, attendance, and homework can be posted for students and parents to look at. The portals are password protected, and only authorized students can access the materials and their grades. This is an advantage for parents, who can also log on at work or at home to check attendance, whether their child's homework is in, or the last test grade. Some portals allow the parents to have a direct connection to the teacher. This virtually brings the classroom home. It also allows schools to have a permanent electronic record of daily classroom activity that provides them with more data about what is happening, or not, in individual classrooms.

Technical staff must have the expertise to advise on whether portals should be produced in-house, be commercially purchased, or be linked by Internet or intranet. They need to arrange for licensing fees, if purchased, or staff time to develop the portals. After the portals are installed, tech staff must work with administration and front-office staff to keep lists of students current and in the correct classes. That can entail a long job. Technical staff need to train teachers and students on how to use the software, check for upgrades, and continually review new products as they come to market.

Timing all of this activity is critical for business managers. Most school budgets are built in the spring for the next academic year. This is also the best time to review with technical staff and individual teachers the plans they have for purchases the next year, grants that they might apply for, and local or national workshops they plan to attend. But when people want to buy and the best time to buy hardly ever coincide. Summer is a busy time for companies and funders to conduct two- to three-week workshops to introduce teachers to new products. Budgets are done in the spring, but in the summer teachers become aware of new products, leaving them with burning pockets when they return in the fall.

In an ideal world, tech staff would keep computers running during the school year and do all new installations, changes to infrastructure, and reimaging in the summer when they have free access to computers without having to compete with students. Reimaging is a suggested annual spring-cleaning of computers. It updates software and gets rid of unauthorized software, including sly spyware and viruses. The result is a perkier computer. Without this being done each year, the computers would become bogged down and slow; operating systems would crash. But in order to reimage, tech staff have to sit in front of the hundred computers in the school. This is the best time to install new hardware and software.

SUMMARY

If all this seems complicated, it does because it is. Each area of school requires different types of computers, auxiliary equipment, software, and Internet access. Matching the type of technology with the purpose of the room is important. The first rooms and computers were one-size-fits-all: get the biggest room and the most screaming computer, and hope that it can deliver what the teachers want. However, this is not an economical or practical method. Some rooms need many computers, some can manage with old computers, and some need powerful machines. The next chapter describes the different types of learning environments and what is needed in each.

Chapter Eleven

Students among the Chaos

The ultimate goal of all educational endeavors is to improve student learning. The big question is, How do you know students have learned or improved? All stakeholders pressure schools to measure and judge the true value of programs, materials, and teaching styles. Like the well-laid-out plans of how teachers were going to use technology with the students, measuring student learning happened, but didn't happen as planned or in as much depth. Knowing how to best serve student learning is always an evolving process as we probe and understand more about the science, physiology, and mechanics of learning. This has been especially true as technology collided with popular culture, widening and deepening the differences between the child and the adult world. Suddenly, the technological world has made children accustomed to a larger virtual world, visually orientated, expectant of instant results, and wildly interactive.

Another example of technology improving learning is computer imaging, which gave new insight into how the brain works and has broadened the definition of intelligence. The brain has been virtually the final frontier for physiology. Until computer imaging, it appeared to be a mysterious ugly, gray, jelly-like mass of stuff with seemingly no movable parts. Pretty icky and not very interesting to dissect, pinch, and prod. One couldn't watch it work. It was thought that children were born with either a good one or a bad one, but either way it was empty of information until someone or something started teaching and dumping in information. All of this dumping was to reach the gold standard of measurement for intelligence, which was how well students did in science and math. Achievement and intelligence test scores were statistics that gamblers could use to predict the probability of a student becoming a physicist. The higher the intelligence score, the more money one could bet.

Actually watching the brain work with computer imaging gave scientists a new perspective on how the brain handles information and develops. The big surprise, scientists found, is that the brain is more developmentally dynamic than was proposed in early learning theories. Most brains don't mature or fully develop until the owners are in their twenties, and even then they can continue to improve and grow smarter. We do use all of our brain. You can teach an old dog to do new tricks. Stroke or accident victims can learn how to recapture the facilities they lost by the brain rearranging its centers and re-connecting synapses. For youth, computer imaging emphasizes the importance of introducing an active-learning atmosphere either at home with a caretaker or through formal experiences in school.

The second realization was that other activities that we once thought were talent, skill, or inheritance, such as language, music, reading, oratory, or sports, are actually highly developed types of intelligence.[1] The brain activity used to process information, organize muscles, and react is all part of a special brain. Few people are going to argue that Einstein was not smart, but so are former president Bill Clinton, former businessperson now philanthropist Bill Gates, actor Robin Williams, and *Harry Potter* author J. K. Rowling. The world is full of smart people who have somehow managed to survive and even succeed without acing calculus and physics, thank heavens. Educators need to cultivate and foster their types of intelligence as well.

Lastly, and most importantly, even if you look at groups of people who achieve in a similar area, their brains work slightly differently because of past knowledge, how they process information, the speed at which they do things, and so on. Brains learn differently, respond at different speeds, and output information differently. Think about putting together a new computer and printer. Some people will open the box and read the directions before they even touch a part, then line up the parts one by one, check the directions, and put them together step-by-step as the directions direct. Others will look at the pictures, only reading if they have an extra part or two. Some people will dump everything on the table and start plugging things in until they get everything to work. If not, and only if they are secure in the finding that a mistake has been made, they will check the directions or pack up everything back in the box, return it to the store, and demand a refund. Others will order a pizza and a cou-

---

1. In 1983, Howard Gardner proposed the theory of multiple intelligences, opening up discussion of new ideas on how children learn and how teachers should teach. This bashed the one-teaching-style-fits-all model that behavioralists were so comfortable with, a theory that rose from Skinner's work with laboratory rats. Gardner's first book, *Frames of Mind*, outlined the theory and introduced the soon-to-be-controversial ideas, and the next book, *Theory of Multiple Intelligences*, published in 1993, refined the theory, and it gained popularity and validity. Now many authors and scientists continue to add on to the idea of students with different learning styles. The current educational buzzword is *differentiated learners*.

ple of six-packs of beer and call their buddies to put it together as they lean over their shoulders and shout encouragement. These are just a few examples of the differences in how students input, process and output information.

And there are brains with serious challenges. People do have learning disabilities that complicate the learning process, and they have brains that have to be outsmarted in order to manipulate and process information. Learning disabilities do not mean that a student cannot learn; it just means he or she has to find a way to get around, depending on the severity, annoyances or major hurdles. Charles Schwab,[2] CEO of the largest brokerage firm; David Boies, lawyer and runner-up in 2000 for *Time* magazine's Man of the Year; Dr. John (Jack) Horner,[3] a dinosaur hunter and advisor to Steven Spielberg on films such as *Jurassic Park* and *The Lost World*; and Robert Benton, a three-time Academy Award–winning screenwriter and director, are all learning disabled. They seemed to have done well for themselves.

All of this challenged the foundation of learning theory; hence, educators began to question what students really were learning, who could learn, and if they could learn more or better. Educators are in the preparation stages of translating what is being discovered in neurobiology and converting the knowledge to experimentation with learning techniques in the classroom. Computers added to teaching myriad variables that are hard to control. They simultaneously expedite and frustrate the measurement process by adding more opportunities for students while adding more complexity to designing research. However, even if the system had not already been strained by new understanding of learning and new ways of delivering the curriculum, there was an urgency to collect the proof that technology was a better way of teaching in order to justify purchases of millions of dollars of technology, infrastructure, and staff—or, for critics and opponents of technology, to collect proof that it did not work.

Unfortunately, early studies about the effectiveness of teaching with technology were caught up in the process of schools creating a technological infrastructure: wiring, equipment, and adapting facilities rather than exploring how students were learning. This was not counterproductive but necessary; at the same time, it was frustrating because of the general lack of being able to focus on what individual students were really learning. Electronic curriculum,

---

2. Charles Schwab started a nonprofit organization that helps parents who have children with learning disabilities. The names came from his Web site www.schwablearning.com, which has a very long list of famous persons who have learning disabilities.

3. In his book *Digging Dinosaurs: The Search That Unraveled the Mystery of Baby Dinosaurs* Jack Horner writes about this challenges with learning disabilities. Despite having neither a BA nor advanced degrees he is the curator of paleontology at the Museum of the Rockies and holds an endowed chair at Montana State University.

lessons, and textbook supplements, the actual things that produce learning and content, sat in the shadows waiting for the minority of teachers to begin using technology. Many good studies were done but not nearly enough to really understand the myriad benefits of technology in the classroom.

Measuring student learning in a classroom is not as easy as setting up an experiment in a lab. In a lab experiment, you have better control over the variables. If you want to show that one type of suntan lotion blocks sunlight better than another one, you submit the suntan lotions to identical tests. You control the conditions in the lab, the procedure by which you handle the materials, the amount of light, the exposure time, the thickness of lotion application, and so on, eliminating variables until the only difference is the formula of each lotion. That cannot be done with students. There are always annoying variables, and there are some natural aversions to taking students out of the classroom, sticking them in labs, and controlling their lives.

Not all students improved, because not all students make low grades due to lack of intelligence or not working. They have other issues: social pressures, family influence, work, lack of motivation, sports, or simply having other interests that keep them from making better grades. A student talented in art, sports, or music might not choose having an A in science as an educational priority. Some of you are nodding your heads remembering the relief of getting the C in science that made you eligible for an extracurricular activity. These students really muddy the waters of evaluating the effectiveness of a learning program. Students have a much different perspective on school than educators.

To begin an evaluation of a teaching product, it is necessary to look into what other researchers found in previous studies and what statistics have been collected that would give insight into what might be expected. One of the most interesting predications for EL (Exploring Life) came from statistics showing that minorities or students from lower socioeconomic communities generally did not have computers at home. Hypothesizing from these figures, it was expected that these students would be less proficient at using computers. Much had been touted in the press about the digital divide—the divide between those who have computers and those who do not. Federal and state programs quickly responded by creating successful programs for minority-serving schools to obtain equipment, access, and training. But still this home computer thing nagged everyone to suppose there would be a wide difference in the skill level of students. This did not prove to be true.

During one of the first school visits, a group of Hispanic students was observed in the back of the room, typing intensely, hesitating only to glance at the clock and then type faster on the computers. When the teacher was asked what the students were doing, he replied that every day he allowed them to access e-mail before class started. Throughout the next two days, it was observed that students' ability to use computers was not predictable by race, gender, or economic level. At each school, students were asked if they had an e-mail account. Most looked at you as if you were from Mars and said, "Dude?" which translates to *yes*. When they were asked where they had access, they answered at relatives' houses, including grandma's house; before and after school; libraries; Internet cafés; parent's work; community centers; during class; and many other places.

This is not to say that students who did not have computers at home were not disadvantaged; they were. But not having a computer at home didn't seem to be a hurdle to their familiarity or comfort level, just as those students who had home computers were not always proficient. Some students had slow connections, competed with siblings or parents for its use, or were simply not interested. It was surprising to hear students brag that they were not the "computer type" and be proud that they never used them. This suggested two things. One was the importance of students having computer access at school. The second was the importance of libraries and community centers that had free access for students. Without these venues, students who did not have computers at home or those who had to stand in line behind other family members would have been severely disadvantaged.

Teachers who realized that students did have access, maybe not at home but somewhere, began assigning homework in which the students had to use electronic activities. The students could access the Internet-based materials anywhere they could access their e-mail. The trick was that the assignment could not be due the next day. As long as the students had a couple of days to complete an assignment, they could arrange to find access at grandma's, the city library, a friend's house, and so on. If students can check their e-mail, they can complete an assignment. Assigning homework on an Internet-based program was no different from assigning a report that required a book or other resources from the library, but it was even better because the Internet, unlike a library, is open day and night and is not restricted to materials purchased on a budget.

A paradox occurred that was puzzling. Some teachers would not assign the students homework on the Internet, despite the fact that the students were not allowed to take their textbooks home. A phenomenon that is growing too fast is that many schools only have enough textbooks to put in a classroom. As a result, reading the textbook is limited to assigned class time for that subject. Students use their notes and handouts to study at home. The reasoning made no sense since there was a decent probability that the students could access the Internet materials outside of school but zero chance that they could read the textbook. Even knowing this, the teachers would not assign the Internet;

go figure. However, the students knew they could access the activities at home, and many of them did extra reading on their own.

The other prediction from the research literature suggested that boys, spending more time on computers, would be more comfortable using them than girls. It was not so. Being female didn't appear to have much influence on students' comfort levels. Remember the classroom with the computers on the lab benches? Five students would share the computer activities while at the lab bench. In an attempt to find out why a female or male student would take control of the computer via the mouse, interviews asked students why the particular student at the mouse was chosen. Whoever got there first started the computer activities. Gaining control of the mouse seemed to be based more on the juiciness of the gossip slowing students as they moved toward the computers than who might be the most proficient.

As the pilot testing continued, another pattern emerged. The teachers were quick to announce that some of the students were not so thrilled with the idea of using computers and were anxious to talk to the on-site evaluator. The teachers were surprised when the evaluator asked if they were the A students, the students who are successful reading the textbook, memorizing facts, and taking tests. The electronic component was unfamiliar territory to them, a risk in an atmosphere in which they excelled. Remember the different ways in which people would put together a computer and printer, each with their own strategy. It is the same with the ways in which students learn. A students felt comfortable with the textbook because that was how they learned best. They liked the written word, going sequentially through the textbook, and answering the questions.

With each module of Exploring Life pilot test, the students were pretested and post-tested. The testing showed an overall improvement in learning. But that improvement was in one lump group; it didn't show how individual students progressed. What was witnessed during observations and teacher interviews was that the mid-level students, the students who earn Cs, did very well—in some cases, extremely well. Early in the evaluation, a teacher reported a D student advancing to As and Bs on his tests. The student had learning disabilities that slowed his reading and comprehension of the material. The activities and visuals increased his learning pace exponentially. Unfortunately for the student, after the five sample chapters were completed, he had to return to the textbook. The teacher reported the sad results: he slid back to the D level. Unfortunately for him, only the trial chapters were online.

It is a bit off topic but thought provoking to note the behavior of another student in the same class, who was very reflective. The student, bent over the computer, would carefully examine the page, taking in every word and activity. When he clicked to go to another section, he would fall back on his chair, extending his arms and palms upward in wonderment at what he was seeing. He was an African boy who had traversed a continent in front of advancing and deadly armies and ravaging predatory animals. Having no family left, the child was fortunate to come to the United States. That particular student humbly reminded us of the luxury and privilege we have in the United States to be able to argue the use of technology in our schools let alone that it is even there.

The progress of learning-challenged students caused the project evaluators to examine how mid-level students, those making Ds and Cs, were progressing. The program was built to employ inquiry, a teaching technique in which students are presented with problems to solve so they can teach themselves basic concepts. Rather than straight lectures, the students were challenged to explore. The electronic activities added visuals for students who needed to see pictures first. The software also had repetitive activities. Students could repeat a concept until they understood it. The software also had well-conducted behavioralist activities. When the students correctly answered a question or put something in order, they were rewarded with sound and images that reinforced what they had learned.

Students whose second language was English also did well. These students most likely learn by looking at pictures or doing activities first. For example, in one class made up largely of Hispanic second language students, the teacher had the students read a section and answer the questions. There were spaces for the students to type in the answers and check them automatically; however, the teacher had them write the answers down on a piece of paper before they checked them. The room slowly sobered down as the students struggled with writing. The answers were slow to write, and, after a half hour, the students had only completed a few questions. They were learning very little science and enjoying it less.

Finally, the evaluator intervened and asked the teacher if the students could go to another section. There, the students had similar questions but in a game format. They were given a short question. They could choose from an array of short answers and immediately discover if they were right or not. The tone and enthusiasm of the class changed as the students challenged each other to get the correct answer. It is undeniable that the students needed to write more, but they also needed to learn science. This quick activity helped them memorize and learn the science terms that they needed.

In a science class, students will learn as much new vocabulary as in a language class. There is no easy way to obtain vocabulary. It must be memorized. Behavioralist learning techniques that employ rewards and immediate feedback are optimal for memorization. Because electronic delivery offers many different types of activities, students who have difficulty memorizing or need help reading can find activities that meet their learning style and level. The Internet portion of EL is huge. There are many more activities than a teacher can do in one year. This is an advantage of electronic delivery: there are few size restrictions. Content and activities do not have to be limited to a paper book that has to be delivered cross-country in trucks, carried in a backpack, or stored during the summer.

Exploring Life did something that textbooks don't do by offering students a choice of activities and the opportunity to self-identify activities at different levels and match them to their academic ability. It was interesting to watch when teachers gave the students an assignment and adequate free time in which to choose activities. There were students who repeated animated demonstrations over and over again until they understood the concept. Some students like the matching. Other students did the activities but kept the book open and followed along with both. Some students liked the activities where when they answered questions they found out immediately if they were right or wrong. Some students never read a word of text, searching for the animated demonstrations and activities; others carefully read and completed activities in sequential order. There were even some old-school holdouts, students who hardly ever used the computer because they didn't want to.

Along with measuring content knowledge gain, the student pretesting and post-testing looked at the students' attitude toward using technology. The students' attitude always measured high, but the surprising finding was that the students' attitude on the post-test was not as high as on the pretest. Because the students seemed to enjoy using the computers so much, this was unexpected. The evaluators investigated this further. As using computers became more of an everyday activity, the novelty factor wore off. Using the computers didn't mean a charge down the halls, an unexpected change from routine, or a stolen opportunity to check e-mail. It was not a day away from the classroom or a special activity that did not count on the test, it was part of the routine of learning. This sobered the students, who enjoyed the party-hearty atmosphere that a computer day created.

On many levels, it was amusing in hindsight to think that there were even questions about students' attitude toward using computers. Computers were as much as a part of their world as chewing gum. Not all were as comfortable as others were, not all were as skilled or knowledgeable, but the real gap existed between their attitudes and the attitudes of teachers. Teachers were being trained to use this new technology. At the same time, the students were growing up with it, and it was a natural part of their environment.

During the pilot testing, many problems occurred. A school computer is not like a home computer. When there is a problem on a home computer, it can be quickly diagnosed. It is a problem with your computer, your service provider, or the Web site. It's pretty simple. School computers are not as simple because there are many layers in which things can go wrong. A problem could occur because of the service provider, too many computers coming online at once, the filtering software, the wrong plug-in, the wrong chip speed, the program being down, and so on.

When problems occurred, the process was to find out the cause. The procedure was to logic it out. For example, if none of the computers could access the program, then it was a problem with housing at EL. If all of the computers could access the program but not the activities on certain chapters, then they did not have Flash. If the activities in chapter 6 did not work but the rest did, then they did have Flash but did not have the latest version of Flash. If the Internet came on in a wave, one computer at a time, then there was a problem with the way the room was wired. If the Internet was sluggish on all the computers, then the schools pipe was not big enough to handle the traffic.

The culture of teachers was drastically altered with the introduction of computers. Teachers were fighting culture shock, but that was not true of students. Students quickly embraced the communication and gaming tools computers offered and entrenched them into their culture while teachers still had the deer-in-the-headlights look. The students had an amazing way of paying no heed to the panic and flurry the teacher, evaluator, and tech staff created as they did problem solving. When things went wrong, students fixed them without hesitation or reflection. This exasperated the elimination steps of the logical process of problem solving. In one classroom in a new school that had new laptops and a more-than-adequate connection, the activities would not work, but there was no general pattern. A couple of computers could access everything, some up to chapter 5. Others could access the program but not the activities. Then some magically behaved.

It was discovered that some of the students, when they were unable to do activities, knew to check the upgrades on the plug-ins and automatically downloaded it, right through the filters and blocks for downloads. The laptops had been checked out from media services, and, even though they were housed in rolling cabinets that contained a classroom set of twenty-five computers, media people would loan out ten here, three here, and twenty over there. When they were returned, they were filed in whatever dock was handy. In the travels from classroom to classroom, each individual computer ended up with different applications or plug-ins. Some of the computers had the correct version of Flash, some had none, and some had the older version. Some of them had Windows Media Player, some had QuickTime. Though the expected constant was that all the computers would be set up with the same applications, this was not true. The students-turned-technicians complicated things further.

The students were more apt to use the electronic components just as they used the Web. They instinctively knew there would be interactives and would rapidly search EL to get things rockin'. They would then, if they had time, go back and look at the text. Long explanations, directions, or oratories were quickly skipped over. In fact, unnecessary text annoyed the students. The trial-and-error method of using the activities would prevail. For some teachers, who were used to the control of a textbook, this was uncomfortable territory. When students were pressed to use the electronic activities in a linear format, with everyone doing the activities together, many of them glazed over.

But not all the students loved using the electronic activities or liked the choices that were offered. Unfortunately, the evaluation investigated why students liked the electronic format, not why they did not prefer it. However, when the concept that some students were more comfortable in a print-text environment is applied to the learning theory that students are different and they learn in diverse ways, it makes perfect sense that some would prefer print. When schools purchase leaning programs, what needs to be understood better is the blend that is needed between different learning styles.

SUMMARY

It is common-knowledge cocktail-party conversation that students are more technologically savvy than many children and young adults. However, this is not a valid argument and is a misconception. Adults do ask younger people to help set up a computer, download new editions, or help them use a new e-mail package. It is often heard from a parent that "Johnny is a computer genius." Translated correctly, this means Johnny spends hours playing on a computer. Young people are glued to pop-cultural activities like MySpace, YouTube, e-mail, discussion groups, and games. However, that is completely different from being able to use technology for learning or mastering employment-related skills. Filming friends acting silly with a cell phone and uploading it to YouTube is not rocket science. But kids need schools to guide them how to use technology for learning. What is different for teachers is that this bombardment of pop cultural influence in students' free time has also affected how they learn and interact with computers. Teachers see curling up with a good book or meeting friends for dinner at the local pub. Students have the same depth of experience and feeling of comfort sitting in front of their computer interacting with friends and resources across the world.

Advanced learning theories show that students have different ways of learning and that teachers who have thirty students in a classroom need to vary the ways in which they teach and assess student progress. Technology is a great tool for accomplishing this. It does not require radical change in teaching practices, but it requires tweaking and modification of what is already in the schools and more informed decisions of what is added and where it is used. The data collected from federal, state, and classroom assessments provides more information for schools to develop programs that fit individual learning styles as well as identify where the entire student body needs to be. To achieve this, business managers need to work with teachers and support staff to locate the tools to diagnose student and school needs and to design programs that achieve the desired result.

There are many more new elements to learn about as students become more and more wired. Students organize their social groups differently because, as teachers discovered with early listservs, they can align themselves with like-minded people from all over the world.

Chapter Twelve

Matching Technology
with the Learning Environment

Equipping computers for all areas of the school can be needlessly expensive, even wasteful, if not governed and managed well. The choice of what to purchase for all the teachers and staff is made simpler and more cost-effective when the teaching goal or function of each area is first clarified and then a strategic plan on how that goal will be met is formulated. That plan, matched with the type of facility available, the best arrangement of computers and auxiliary equipment, and the needed software or applications will guide appropriate technology choices that are tailored to each area of the school's specific requirements. An important consideration for business managers is that thoughtful decisions about where and how to use computers throughout the school can save on licensing fees, equipment, and maintenance.

There are many considerations that need to be taken into account in order to determine the best technologies for each area of the school. The upcoming examples show how teachers were able to creatively consider the facilities and their budgets to find a way to use technology to improve their teaching. They show that there are many ways to mix technology to meet a teaching goal.

THE CENTRAL OFFICE

The central office is the heart of communication within the school and in the community.[1] Most schools are saving trees and labor costs by communicating with teachers and staff via e-mail or Web pages on the Internet or intranet

---

1. To clarify, in this book the central-office computers include those for administrators, clerical support staff, and teachers who serve in an administrative capacity.

rather than via mailboxes or flyers posted in the lounge. The school Web site, commonly managed by the front office, is an important venue for informing the community about sports, concerts, plays, parent meetings, and special events. It is the central clearinghouse for data collection. The front office is the center for most of the ordering and receiving of equipment, supplies, and materials. All of these functions are made easier by technology and the networking of the school's computers.

Technology is a backup for those newsletters and flyers that students carefully wad up and cram into the scary depths of their black-hole backpacks. Information can economically be sent via e-mail or put on the Web site as a failsafe measure so that caregivers can actually see what their students meant to take home or what they errantly buried in a pile of papers somewhere in the kitchen, den, or bathroom. Not to be outdone, teachers and staff have about the same luck as students and parents in preserving newsletters. When schools have an electronic system where central office staff can post information, caregivers can check for information at home, from work, or wherever. They are unlikely to misplace their office computers.

Often, the school's Web site is created and managed from the central office. Although the Web site does not necessarily need a high-end computer or software, it does need high-end attention. To the outside world, the Web site is the school's visual identity. It is an important community public-relations tool that can frame positive attitudes toward the school or, if badly constructed and badly maintained, can foster negative attitudes. Taxpayers, community members, parents, and students will all make judgments about the quality and attitude of the school according to the effectiveness of the visual presentation. The Web site is the first thing jobseekers see when they look for a community in which to purchase a home or business. First impressions are very important to creating lasting positive attitudes.

There is another powerful use of the Web page, and that is the attraction of outside funders. They will often even make judgments on whether or not the school can manage the money or technology they give based on the visual identity and attention to detail. Private or industrial funders will evaluate the Web page to determine if they would want the school representing their cause, initiative, or product. They want a role model, an exemplary school that will encourage others to further the funder's cause or purchase their product. Many companies give to local schools with the alternative motive of establishing community goodwill. The money comes from the public-relations, human-resources, or advertising budget. The purpose is to earn a positive corporate identity in the neighborhood or region in which they have branches or a national office. They want the school to reflect the quality of the industry. An attractive and updated Web page can further a school's chances of appealing to outside funders.

Another important task for the front office is data collection and dissemination. All the central-office computers need to be networked on the school's secure intranet. This makes data collection more efficient because teachers and staff can input information directly into their classroom computers and, with a click, sent it to the central office. Data entered this way is more reliable because it does not depend on a person recording secondhand or tardy information. Lunch count can go directly to the cafeteria, attendance can go straight to the principal, and student visits to the nurse or counselor are confidential without the danger of extra eyes transporting or misplacing paper copies. Once the front office has collected and compiled the information, it can be sent to the district or state offices via the Internet. If the school includes Internet access to the intranet, parents or caregivers can know within minutes via e-mail or a secure portal if their child is not in school, is missing a class, or didn't submit his or her homework.

All of this is possible; however, software needs to be purchased or written to accomplish this. Secure networks have to be maintained. Most importantly, the information must be collected in a form that is compatible in terms of operating systems, data collection software, plug-ins, and so on with all of the computers within the school, including those in the counselor's office, nurse's office, facilities, classrooms, and libraries. It also has to be compatible with the computers at the collection institution but still allow the school flexibility to add to data they may want to collect. At the same time, business managers and tech staff should keep an eye on the future to allow the school to collect additional data that it needs as diagnostic information for administrative effectiveness or to improve student learning. Therefore, the system should be expandable and not be a dead end for progress.

The money for administrative computers is most often considered an operating cost, is usually a line item on the budget, and therefore is a priority technology and software purchase for the school. In order to make sure all the schools are using the same hardware and software, many states will earmark money for front-office computers from the funds they distribute. They do this to ensure that the proper equipment and software are purchased because it is very rare that schools obtain outside funding for operating costs like they do for enhancement programs. Funders are leery and apprehensive of giving money directly to operating costs because there is less accountability and the gift is often seen as a small fish lost in the vast and swirling ocean of general funds.

The technology needs of the central office include computers for word processing: generating correspondence, forms, newsletters, flyers, spreadsheets, and even posters. Even though these documents may contain pictures and graphics, the memory and speed requirements are low. Within most situations, a common application suite of word-processing programs and less-powerful computers can handle most of the front office's needs, including the graphics and images needed for that level of work. Publishing software purchased independently or in a suite of office applications allows front-office staff to easily create professional-looking newsletters, flyers, and other documents, which are sent out into the community, to parents, and to district and state offices.

- technology: desktop basic productivity, secure high-speed connection to the Internet and intranet, server
- applications: word-processing suite, publishing software and Web software if not included in the word-processing suite, PDF reader and generator
- software: data-collection software if the state or district does not supply a data-collection system, manager access to classroom-manager software
- networking: Internet, intranet, and extranet connections; e-mail; Web site
- plug-ins and downloads: browser, Flash or other animation software, multimedia player
- training: word processing, Web and paper publishing, spreadsheets

LIBRARY

Of all the areas that use computers, the library is probably the support service that has been most empowered, has increased in importance, and has broadened its role and accountability in student learning. Too many readers of this book can remember being assigned a report and looking up a country, animal, or topic in a bound paper encyclopedia only to discover that the information is almost a decade old and the initials of one's older sister and her boyfriend are scribbled on every other page until the big breakup. It was very frustrating. Even when the information was current, the lack of other resources and the impressively displayed bound books seemed dogmatic; the encyclopedia was the ultimate, indisputable source of reliable information. There was little chance to look up other resources or to get a different perspective from various debating authorities. The students' reports were carbon copies of each other, and it is not surprising that students thought books held ironclad facts, not ideas, informed opinions, or evolving data. The information age changed that.

Schools have always been limited by space and budgets from having a wide variety of resources and books. There were never enough books at the appropriate reading level, enough variety in topics, or even enough copies of a popular book. If students were to be investigative and lifelong learners, they needed to know how to use search tools. Do the numbers here. If education is to instill a love of reading, then students need something to read. Reading materials need to be in the hands of students. Too often, library books had gone the way of textbooks and were too precious or scarce for students to take outside of the school. The library became a museum of books. The information age changed that.

Electronic references, Web sites, and electronic books enhance libraries by making a wide variety of books available electronically. Electronic books can be downloaded for checkout to students' computers, cell phones, PDAs, and iPods. Unfortunately, like e-textbooks and for similar reasons, e-books have yet to make it big. They are even duller on a computer or handheld monitor than they are on paper. The biggest advantage is that they can be read at a dark restaurant when one is caught alone for dinner. E-books and e-textbooks do little to take advantage of the interactivity of the Internet. All this will change soon with advanced technology, but the biggest expansion of the libraries is in the resources it can offer and the information-management expertise of librarians. Librarians have always been in the business of information management; however, there was a lack of available information for them to manage. The Internet has changed that just in time. Libraries now play a much more prominent role in producing students who meet the needs of employers.

Employers want to hire people who have problem-solving skills and can solve problems using technology. For example, at one time bevies of bookkeepers were needed by retail stores to take the receipts from each store and accurately and neatly post data manually into general ledgers. Remember teachers grading handwriting? Now salesclerks at stores in Atlanta or Philadelphia enter transactions into cash registers-turned-computers. The data flies over the Internet and is automatically compiled in the electronic ledgers in San Diego. The job responsibility of the bookkeeper is to solve problems like checking for inaccuracies in the data, finding entry mistakes, and posting changes. Because bookkeepers don't have to do the tedious and time-consuming data entry, other tasks like running payroll or billing were added to their jobs. Fewer bookkeepers are needed to do more tasks, and the skills schools need to foster in students are critical thinking and problem solving.

Teachers and libraries need to collaborate to create the type of instruction and training the students need in order to be information managers, critical thinkers, and problem solvers. Librarians have advanced training in information management. Teachers can't be familiar with all the databases, journals, government documents, and Internet search engines that students need to do investigative work. Teachers are content providers and foster critical-thinking skills in students. By teaming with librarians, teachers can send students with critical-thinking skills to learn how to access information and then manage it.

For example, to build analytical skills and solve real problems, students must be able to hypothesize probable solutions and then access information, evaluate its validity, and apply it appropriately. If a student wants to write a paper on the environment, he or she needs to know more than how to put *environment* in a browser and wade through the gazillion references that pop up. Research in the information age is a science and a trained skill. It is not a skill that students build in one trip a year to the library.

Libraries may look different for lower-level grades because it is hard to imagine why third graders would be left to wander around the Internet, even as skilled investigators, when most of the material would be over their reading, academic, or interest level. They would not be able to filter material to their level of understanding. Elementary-school librarians may have different missions, which are influenced by the students' academic and community socioeconomic level. The business manager, teachers, and support staff will need to discuss what information-management skills and exposure their students need. They can then plan where, at what level, and how the library will meet those needs and how the library will be integrated into the curriculum.

For example, the goal in an elementary-school library in an underserved community where students don't have books at home may be to foster in the students a love of reading. The school may choose to meet this goal by having the librarians write interactive online tailored materials that direct the students to reading materials that excite them. The librarians use their information-management skills to search for appropriate materials and build the virtual library on a secure portal students can access during and after school. Together, business managers, teachers, and librarians can work with companies or their own tech staff to build the type of information-management system students need so they can be safe and smart on the Internet.

Libraries at the upper grade levels will want to fine-tune the skills students need for college and work. To do this, business managers along with teachers and support staff can plan ways to regularly integrate the library into more classes. It is well understood that the majority of schools do not currently have professionally trained librarians because they are scarce and expensive. However, just like technology created the need for technical support staff, expanding the role of libraries will also create a need and hence funds for professional staff. Business managers will be challenged with discussions on whether the school should hire a degreed librarian or devote more budget money toward professional development for currently employed librarians.

Think of information management as an additional subject, not an add-on to the English teacher's instructional activities. A high-school teacher can have a hundred to two hundred students all needing constant feedback about their writing, spelling, and grammar. An example of how an English teacher and librarian can partner is that the English teacher can give all his students an assignment to write a descriptive paper. His expertise and skill is in explaining the concept, describing the assignment, working with students through their drafts, and providing feedback on spelling, grammar, and the logical presentation of the material. The library is where students receive guided and knowledgeable instruction on how to do a search on a specific database or over the Internet. The librarian will also help the students to manage and filter the information they find to present a logical and informed line of reasoning in their papers.

To match environment with learning, business managers will want to discuss with librarians and facilities staff how to best arrange the library technology for the most users. There needs to be a set of computers for reference in view of the librarian or trained staff so they can help individual students and teachers who are doing research on their own. There also needs to be a classroom where librarians can instruct at one time twenty or thirty students in a class who are doing a specialized search for a project or paper. Libraries are often the place where teachers check out equipment like slide, film, and LCD projectors and laptop computers. It's a busy place. Business managers will need to work with librarians and facilities staff to plan how all these activities can take place.

But not all information resources are free. Many of the subscription databases require a yearly fee, and it can be quite substantial. This requires the business manager to work with librarians and teachers to prioritize which databases would be the most beneficial to the entire school. Many states are organizing consortiums of libraries, which reduce the fee. Partnerships with local, state, and university libraries can be arranged to gain access to databases. Technology for libraries is very fundable from outside sources. Libraries are high profile, have many users, and are often centrally located in the schools. Librarians are trained in Web site development. All of these factors are the sizzle funders look for.

- technology: desktop basic productivity, high-speed connection to the Internet
- applications: Web software, PDF reader and generator, basic word-processing and spreadsheet applications
- databases: as determined by teachers and librarians
- networking: Internet, Web site, and intranet for librarians
- plug-ins and downloads: browser, animation software, and multimedia player

LARGE COMPUTER LABS

The environment of computer labs physically restricts students and limits the type of activities that can be done successfully. In order for the school to get thirty or more computers in one room, students are locked into the computer with little working area to place materials and resources. The narrow aisles prohibit students from being arranged in groups or walking around the room in any way other than single file. The constant background noise of the equipment and the lack of eye contact with students limit the amount of talking the teacher can do or the verbal directions he or she can give. That being said, there are other types of activities that can be done extremely well in this environment.

Labs excel when students are engaged in a computer activity for the entire period, there is limited whole-group instruction or discussion, and students work on their own. Activities that fit the environments of labs are learning keyboarding or other skills that require practice—students just pounding repetitively away for the entire period. Like learning a musical instrument, mastering keyboarding just takes practice. Other examples are programs that are self-paced, where students work independently at their own academic speed the entire period. They interact with the teacher on a one-on-one basis when they need help. Another example occurs when students receive group instruction in a traditional classroom and then are rotated to the computer lab to do activities or practice what they have learned. For example, an English teacher might explain concepts and ideas on Monday and Tuesday and have students work on their drafts and final papers Wednesday through Friday. The students can individually go to the teacher for assistance.

Labs are most often financed under operating costs. Most states require that students demonstrate computer literacy, and therefore they provide funding for labs. Labs aren't as attractive for outside funders, but if a school has a room and doorway there is space to put a donor's name. Unlike projects done by individual teachers, labs are permanent and don't rely on a teacher or program. They have the sustainability that funders like. They can go back from year to year to see their named lab room. This permanence also makes it easier to go back to the funder every couple of years to upgrade computers in lieu of the latest technology.

- technology: desktop basic productivity
- applications: basic word processing and spreadsheets, other office application programs, and applicable software
- networking:
    - Internet is optional depending on the types of classes taught
    - computer networking within the room is advised so that computers are networked to the teacher's computer and the student computers can be controlled (frozen) for lectures
    - intranet if students are using course-management software
- plug-ins and downloads

SPECIALTY LABS

Large schools can often dedicate labs to one subject; for example, computer literacy, language arts, or English. Students will fill them up almost every period. The best part is that when they are empty they can be reserved by teachers in the same or other disciplines on an as-needed basis. Some of the large specialty labs are easily funded by grants. However, it becomes awkward if the lab is so specialized or limited by the promises to the grant funders that it ends up empty for much of the day. For example, in one observed school, which had a large population of ESL students, a language lab was completely empty because the teacher who built the lab moved to another school. The promise to the funders was that it would be reserved just for ESL classes, and the equipment was so expensive that the school dared not risk bending the rules. The hiring process for finding a teacher to run the lab was slow, and a substitute could not be found. Hence, the lab was abandoned until the hiring process was complete, which did not happen that semester.

CLASSROOMS

Classrooms are a virtual free-for-all. First, the technology in classrooms is guided and justified by the learning goals and objectives of the students. That means that every teacher or group of teachers organized by grade level or discipline needs to assess where their students are and what they need to do to bring them to excellence. Because there is such a wide spectrum of what technology can produce and how it can deliver the curriculum, there is no set formula. Second, electronic curriculum for learning is still an unknown. There needs to be more experimentation to determine how this is going to play out and mature. This is going to be expensive. An example is using tablet computers that are connected to the teacher's computer for math so the teacher can easily check individual students' process as they are solving problems. Others are testing students online so they can grade and provide feedback to students. This is something that one teacher who has two hundred students a day cannot do. Technology allows teachers to check student progress more often so they can catch misconceptions and students who are struggling.

Many subjects, like art, music, and computer science, use software or applications that do require screaming machines to handle graphics, video, programming, and other specialty programs. Getting these machines is a bit more than getting a free kitten. It is more like receiving a free lion. They often require auxiliary equipment that is also expensive to purchase, protect, and maintain. That being said, they are completely necessary for upper-level students in some disciplines. For example, in the introductory art classes, students need to first understand the basic concepts of color, design, and creativity. However, for students to be employable or gain entrance to college they need to have a demonstrated ability in computer-generated art. It is value added. Sometimes decisions to purchase computers for advanced students are going to have to be made.

SUMMARY

Business managers need to work with teachers, librarians, and support staff to match the correct mix of environment, technology, and learning programs and not think of the classroom as the only place for supporting learning and skill acquisition. Putting appropriate technology in the correct environment will not entail catastrophic change; rather, it will entail fine-tuning of what is already occurring. The front office can be the arm of public relations and institutional development by using computers to create the school's visual identity to the outside world. Libraries are seeing new crowds of students who were once absent. Students may be coming to use e-mail, MySpace, and other pop-culture applications, but they are coming. Industry is demanding that students be proficient in information management, and with technology, librarians have the tools to make this happen. Business managers need to mediate among teachers and support staff to determine the most efficient and cost-effective areas to begin experimenting with electronic curriculum and to place computers that match the teaching objectives.

Chapter Thirteen

Before Buying Technology

Purchasing electronic curriculum involves many more wide-ranging decisions than purchasing a textbook. The process for deciding what textbook to adopt and purchase is already established in the system. This is a generic description but will work to explain the system: the textbook committee meets, they argue, they decide on a text, 40 percent of the committee members pout, and the chosen textbook gets ordered and delivered, and they open the boxes. No one has to come in and fix a textbook. The school does need to replace those that are lost, stolen, or fall apart. Someone does have to collect them at the end of the year, notify parents or guardians if the books are lost or damaged, and pile them up to store over the summer. It is a clerical job that doesn't need teacher or professional staff support but sometimes becomes part of their jobs. But, even with all this, textbooks don't need the type of support that electronic curriculum demands. A textbook doesn't rely on support staff on a constant or even daily basis like technology does.

Most schools adopt textbooks every five to eight years. One year they may adopt science books, another year math books, so that each year the textbook for a discipline or grade is replaced or renewed. A school could have as many as a hundred genres and types of textbooks, so this round-robin keeps the adoption system manageable. This way there are always new books coming in and some going out so the students don't have all used books. Once a book is adopted, the publisher will keep that edition available for the length of the adoption so schools can purchase replacement copies. Textbooks do fade away and become obsolete and dog-eared.

The pace at which missing textbooks are replaced is the decision of administrators and sometimes teachers but is always conditional on the budget. In the observed schools, not all schools replaced texts regularly, especially when they neared the end of the adoption period. Many schools only had classroom sets, stored on shelves or under the desks for the students to use during class time. When this happens, students are not allowed to take books home and usually work from their notes or worksheets. Some schools will only allow students to take a book home if they have a signature from a caretaker guaranteeing that they will replace the book if lost, stolen, or destroyed.

Unlike purchasing textbooks, purchasing electronic curriculum requires participation and input from others besides teachers. This is because the questions and solutions will need to consider differential learning—the diverse ways in which students learn—and which strategies are most appropriate. Decisions will also be guided by student, teacher, and school data available for diagnosing unique learning challenges that may change from year to year. Business managers must work with teachers to identify specific pedagogical needs, establish learning goals, and support their pedagogical plans. Then business managers and teachers need to consult with technology or other support staff to determine how the learning goals will be accomplished.

Business managers and teachers should not think of technology integration and electronic curriculum as a replacement for a textbook. Textbooks do a fine job. However, daily instruction using technology can broaden the opportunities for students who don't learn well by reading. Electronic curriculum can add reinforcing interactives, provide quizzes that give immediate feedback, individualize lessons, and even talk to the students. It does not necessarily mean the death of textbooks, It means using the learning goal to dictate the types of teaching tools that will be used. For some students and situations, textbooks will be the answer.

Because technology infrastructure is becoming a commodity, teachers can do what they were not able to do before: diagnose and say what they want technology to do. Buying computers, teacher training, and building infrastructure are no longer leading technology purchases; pedagogy is. Business managers are needed to assist teachers and staff as they do this. Below is a list of questions business managers may want to encourage teachers to pose before they purchase any type of learning tool.

WHAT IS THE PROGRAM EXPECTED TO ACCOMPLISH?

The answer to this question is the first thing teachers need to consider. A hypothetical example is that the data collected from classroom daily grades and state achievement tests may show that the students in the third grade are poles apart in their reading ability, ranging from a high to a low level. The reasons for this can be myriad: students whose second language is English, learning disabilities, or just not enough practice reading outside of school. Whole-group instruction, the entire class doing the same thing together, is very difficult when some students are struggling and others are bored. It is also hard to productively occupy students while the teacher gives attention to small groups or individual students. Lastly, increasing the students' and teacher's frustration, a single reading textbook may be too difficult for lower-level students and not difficult enough for advanced students.

A group of teachers wants to purchase an electronic reading program for the entire third grade so that students can work individually and begin the program at their own levels, competing against themselves to raise their scores. This way the teacher can pull out certain students for remedial or advanced help. This goal may be achieved through a commercial purchase or through teachers and tech staff designing a program that allows self-paced instruction for individual students, which a teacher can use to keep all the students engaged and learning while he or she acts as a facilitator to help students individually or in small groups.

WHAT HAVE OTHER SCHOOLS EXPERIENCED?

After identifying the goal, the teachers' first steps would be to research if other schools have experienced the same challenge and then to learn what commercially or academically produced programs they found that work. Because most federal- and state-funded projects require that recipients publish their results, this information can be found in the educational literature. The most common place this information is found is in academic and practitioner journals accessed through the library's databases. But research and reports of programs can also be found free on the Internet using a browser. Web software, blogs, and discussion groups have made it easy for educators to publish information directly to the Internet rather than going through the lengthy process of paper publishing. Online newspapers like *The New York Times'* education edition and other news services like www.edweek.org have articles about what schools are doing.

After similar schools and authors of papers or postings are identified, teachers can use e-mail to communicate with each other. They can share information about what strategies they have been using and exchange best practices. However, teachers should be cautious of others who declare their programs successful on anecdotal information alone. The important point is to understand how they established the effectiveness of the program. What measurement instruments did they use? How many students were involved? What was the effect on students' performance? If the program was not successful, find out the pitfalls of the project and the regrets of the teachers.

After the teachers are informed about what works and what does not, they can better research in depth the types of commercially or academically produced programs that match their goals. Another option would be to investigate the pursuit of grant funds to produce tailored materials with a local university or a partnership with one of the schools to expand their data on learning. At this stage, armed with information, teachers can begin meeting with the business manager and technical staff to strategically plan what will best suit the students, budget, and technical support and what purchases would meet the learning goals. But there are still more questions to ask.

HOW WILL THE TEACHER
OR TEACHERS USE THE PROGRAM?

If the program is to be used with students, is the program flexible enough that it can be used in many ways: in the classroom, in other school facilities, or by the students at home? Programs that are flexible in the way they can be used are very often the better buy. For example, both GSLC (Genetic Science Learning Center) and EL (Exploring Life) can be used in different ways. The teachers can use classroom presentation equipment and use the material as a demo to enhance lectures. They can also organize the students into small groups of three or four to a computer to complete the activities. Students can also use the activities individually, working on computers in a lab. Finally, students can use either program out of class as homework.

An added flexibility of the EL program was that it had already assembled and matched a textbook, hands-on labs, and electronic activities. The teachers could pick and choose according to what type of teaching technique was appropriate. They could do a hands-on activity, read the textbook, or do something online. They did not have to search around for a hands-on activity that would match what the students were learning online or reading from the text. There were also a lot of electronic activities at a wide variety of levels.

Another question to consider is whether one teacher will use the program or whether it will be adopted with other teachers in the same grade level or discipline. For example, both GSLC and EL were pilot tested by individual teachers; however, in some schools other teachers began adopting the same program. However, there were problems when teachers, who often inherited the old equipment from early adopters, did not have adequate or reliable access. This is where there needs to be mediation from the business manager. It is kind of fair play to allow the early adopters to struggle with something they want to do that is out of step with the school. When the second wave comes in, the rules change. Equity has to be considered.

If the program will be adopted by all the teachers in, let's say, the fourth grade, then there needs to be some discussion about the number of computers and facilities that will be devoted to the project. This is a similar challenge to the challenge that hands-on science labs faced. Is it possible to put a lab in each classroom or make one large lab that the teachers can share on a rotating basis? Can laptops be purchased and rotated between classrooms? Or is it possible to have presentation equipment in each classroom and have the students access the program on their own for homework or personal use? This process is similar to what the early adopters did with GSLC and EL. They adapted the program to fit their circumstances. Creativity is the key.

Even if an identical set of computers is purchased for each teacher, early adopters will continue to seek out additional technology. For example, classroom sets of laptops might be purchased for all the teachers, but the early adopter, delighted but not content with just one technology, charges ahead and begins to experiment with something new he or she saw at a conference. Mediation ensures that the teachers all have fair and equal access to computers that will run the program but still allows the early adopters the support and freedom to do their thing.

If an entire grade or discipline is going to adopt the program, there is another consideration. Some teachers are not going to use technology even if they have a complete setup in the room. Just as not all students feel comfortable and competent learning with technology, not all teachers will use technology. The same academic freedom that allows teachers to use technology allows them to not use technology. And whether they use it or not, there will be plenty of students to match their teaching style. Therefore, it is important that the students be able to have access on their own during free time at school or outside of school.

Don't discount the initiative of and interest from students. Even without any encouragement, students will use educational materials for their own edification. In pilot testing of both GSLC and EL, students were active users without teacher intervention. Parents also like to access materials their children are using. For a student to be able to use the program independently from the teacher is also value added for students who cannot attend school. They can use the program at home or wherever they are. This way they can keep up with the class during their absence.

IS THE PROGRAM RESTRICTED
TO A SPECIFIC TIME OF YEAR?

This is the age of accountability for schools. State standards, grade-level exit exams, and the No Child Left Behind Act (NCLB) require that teachers cover specific topics that will be on the test. This book will not argue the merits of testing but does point out that teaching to the test exists. Also, although NCLB will be subject to a new administration soon and will most likely take on a new identity, testing of students will not go away. To be sure that certain topics are covered, states, districts, or schools are increasingly mandating a specific time of year when each topic is to be covered. This nonflexible time schedule hampered the pilot testing of both GSLC and EL. For example, GSLC is a program that is most likely to be used during the time that teachers are teaching genetics or cell biology, which is usually at the beginning or end of the year. Therefore, pilot testing was always badly timed because if the time for genetics had passed the teacher did the testing out of generosity.

Timing also needs to be a consideration when purchasing a product. If the teachers want to increase the reading scores of children with a program that requires each student to have access to a computer, then there is another important question. Can the program be purchased, teachers be trained, equipment installed, and rooms altered in time for the program to have an effect on the students before the round of testing? Should the purchase, to the chagrin of the salesperson, be delayed until summer when technical staff can build the classroom infrastructure? Sometimes a delay can put the school in line with a newer edition. Some programs, like EL, can be put in at any time since student use is not restricted to one computer per student or even to the classroom. Business managers will have to consider questions of timing beyond the energy of eager buyers.

All this being said, there is one more important consideration in delaying purchases until technology staff can work on them or equipment can be bought. The rule with both GSLC and EL was that if a teacher used technology, they got technology. At the beginning of both products' tests, few teachers had the equipment needed, but they did at the end. Market forces set in. Without the software, there was no demand. Put exemplary software in the hands of teachers, and technology magically appears. Software leads to technology integration. School infrastructure is advanced enough now that software will lead the next phase of technology integration. Pushing the envelope to enact change is part of our educational system.

HOW MUCH TEACHER TIME
WILL THE PROGRAM REQUIRE?

There are many resources for teachers to use, and they require different amounts of teacher time to alter the materials to be appropriate for the classroom. For example, the Internet is chock-full of teaching resources; however, it is a huge time commitment to find activities and then alter them. Study after study shows that the biggest hurdle for any innovation or change is the lack of teacher time. When the teachers have to fuss with activities to make them age-, achievement level-, and interest-appropriate, the activities will most likely be abandoned, no matter how good they are. Information management can while away hours, and most teachers don't have the time to devote to it. This is where commercially produced electronic curriculum is going to shine.

WHEN IS THE TIME TO BUY?

While we were visiting schools, it was not uncommon to see computers sitting in a classroom, plugs dangling, because the technology staff did not have the time to install software or an upgrade or to run wires and cable. The computers sat there because the technology staff did not have the time or staff to hook everything up. The times when technology money appears, when teachers are anxious to buy, and when schools can accommodate a software or equipment purchase don't always match—okay, so they hardly ever match up. Teachers and many support staff are out for over two months during the summer. Winter holidays, spring break, and other holidays shorten the time for decision making and creating the technology infrastructure. Hence, the decision makers are most active during the academic year from September until May when the technology staff is busiest just keeping computers running. Like kids who get new sleds at Christmas, they want to use their presents right away—snow or no snow.

The time to buy software that will make an infrastructure change is in the spring. The reason spring is important is that it is budget time. In a perfect world, teachers should come back from summer with new ideas, the data numbers for the previous year crunched, and the business manager would have everyone together for discussions. Even though just one teacher may be purchasing a product, it can affect the infrastructure and teaching of the entire school. It is a domino effect. Spring is a mad time because teachers are busy trying to finish out the school year, keeping up with cultural activities like banquets, and not thinking about what they will need for the next year. However, technology staff are thinking about summer, when they shed the franticness of maintenance and finally begin to do the fun part, building infrastructure.

The large textbook companies have years of experience working with schools. They are all over them during the spring. It is positively scary. However, textbook publishers know the importance of a purchase by spring in order to serve the client by fall. They have masked the complexity of printing and shipping and work the system well. The sellers and buyers of technology aren't quite as savvy about the complexity of the timing of a product or the effect it has on the entire school infrastructure. Downloading a program and accessing the Internet appear to be so simple at home or in the office, but they are not simple for schools. Software developers are just beginning to become savvy to this.

WHICH COMPUTERS SHOULD BE PURCHASED?

When business managers and technical staff have a clear understanding of how a computer will be used and what software it will run, it is easier to choose and purchase the most cost-effective one. Computer companies understand their clients' lack of technical knowledge and have a process that walks buyers through a purchase by asking them what the functions are. Clients don't need to know about bytes, RAM, or memory but can build their new computers according to the way in which they will be used. Understanding the need also helps with deciding whether or not used equipment can be salvaged and used effectively rather than purchasing new equipment. For example, for a single-purpose function, new software may run well on retired computers allowing another area of the school to purchase faster and larger computers. Shuffling computers around will take planning and discussion among the technical staff, teachers, and support staff.

Designated computers that just handle one program or application are less expensive and easier to scrounge because they have fewer requirements to fulfill. The same with maintenance—the fewer the uses and users the easier computers are to service. But designated computers are only better if the product the teacher is using will be the same from one year to the next. If the product is special, a beta test, or the teacher's ability to commit to long-term use is limited, designated computers may not work. If the teacher uses a variety of software and Internet programs, then the package, not just one program, has to be considered.

But integration doesn't always mean that there will be a specific program that teachers will use. It could be that basic application programs are what the teacher needs. Most elementary students do not need all the bells and whistles that come with professional office suites. Many of the recycled computers will have applications that students can use without

WHERE WILL THE COMPUTERS BE PLACED?

Even if students need their own computers, there are options. A school may shuffle the rooms, not the computers. An example is the way in which schools made science labs to accommodate the need for students to do hands-on activities; the teachers rotated their classes using one lab. If teachers in one discipline or one grade are going to use the same program, then it might be possible for them to share a computer lab. The downside would be if the school has an extra room or if one teacher agrees to his or her room being the computer lab. Another option is to have shared laptops that can travel from room to room. All of these situations would require strong and skillful mediation.

The other question is How safe is the place where the computers and students are going to be? It is naive to think that electrical strips and extension cords aren't going to be used. However, many of the situations observed were just plain dangerous; over-extended outlets and extension cords running up walls and under students' feet are accidents waiting to happen. At some point, risk-management best practices have to kick in to protect students from injury and the school from liability. When early adopters were plugging into extension cords, it involved one classroom, maybe a couple, but when the majority of teachers are using technology, the situation becomes perilous.

WHAT MINIMAL OPERATING SYSTEM DO THE COMPUTERS NEED?

Upgrades to operating systems are like textbooks: schools only can afford to upgrade every five to eight years. Unlike textbooks, the programs that are produced usually have the newest operating system; therefore, as new computers are purchased, schools have little choice but to use the new operating system. As time marches on, schools could end up with four or more operating systems.

If the school needs to purchase an upgrade or new operating system in order to accommodate a program, then that cost has to be factored in. If the school does purchase a newer operating system, then the problem of teachers who are running old software needs to be factored in. They may be left out of the new operating system or forced to purchase a newer edition or find a new product. Remember the school that upgraded to accommodate EL, causing another teacher not to be able to run her longtime software? This is a common occurrence when computers are scarce and serving many teachers. As schools collect more and more computers, it will be a matter of just leaving some computers behind to run old software or applications.

WHAT SPEED PROCESSOR DO THE COMPUTERS NEED?

All programs want to be able to operate at the speed of light, but not all need to. What processors are truly optimal for the product? If it is a fast-paced, game-like program or large illustration software, then the faster the processor, the better. If it is a program that doesn't require heavy graphics or programs beyond standard software like QuickTime Player or Windows Media Player, then less processor speed is needed.

HOW MUCH MEMORY DO THE COMPUTERS NEED?

Memory becomes an issue when teachers or students want to run many or large programs or applications on the computer. For example, Photoshop is a program that requires a lot of memory to run. If the students want to open graphics, video-editing, and word-processing programs all at once, the computer needs to have more memory than a computer used for just a single purpose. Programs accessed over the Internet require much less memory because the company or host has the entire program on its large computers.

If students want to store their drawings or other work on the computer, it will quickly fill up. Therefore, most students will be required to save their work on disks, flash memory sticks, memory cards, or external hard drives. By the time this book is printed, there will be new storage and memory products. All of these add to the expense of using a computer and will require that tech staff not only keep up with innovations but also evaluate what is economical and cost-effective for use with students. Thirty flash memory sticks can easily walk out of a classroom or be walked on. Again, the question is what teachers want to do. Then decisions can be made as to how it will be accomplished.

Schools that have developed an intranet may want to consider storage on the network for students in all or just upper-level courses. For example, on computers that are linked to the network, students can have accounts where the memory and storage capacity are allotted by the types of courses in which they are enrolled. This eliminates students having to purchase personal memory or the school having to supply it. It also prevents tragedies of lost, stolen, or destroyed work because work is saved on a mobile device. However, this option opens new concerns: security and the purchase of more computers and servers.

Schools may want to archive some information, not just put it into memory. Archiving means that it will be stored permanently for multiple years. Much of the information put into computers may be important to protect but may be easily lost, may be personal data that the owner should take responsibility for, or may be expected to eventually be out of date. For example, a student may be working on an illustration for the January student newspaper and may want to keep the edition online to work on it and, when done, keep it for reference. At some point, the school may want to archive the newspaper as well as independently archive the student's original artwork. Other information that would need to be archived would include student data, classroom records, or any other type of data that needs to be stored for multiple years. Post–Hurricane Katrina, many schools are considering offsite locations for archival data.

HOW FAST ARE UPGRADES COMING?

There are lots of reasons for a company to upgrade products, and the ramifications are not always best for the school. Companies rely on beta testers and first users to find all the bugs in new software. It is not so much a way for the company to save money, as it is just the only way all the bugs are going to be found. The change is to schools is that they get free or reduced-rate programs. On the downside, as bugs are found, software upgrades may not be far behind.

Whether the software is new or old, the school needs to protect itself from mandatory upgrades that happen during the busiest months of the school year. Upgrades have to be scheduled when tech staff has time to devote to them. When the students are in the classroom, there is little opportunity for doing anything except keeping everything operating. Consideration has to be given to how the technology staff would have to do the upgrade. Is it a simple push to all computers, or will tech staff have to personally upgrade each computer? The school also has to protect itself from upgrades that pass on unnecessary costs to the school. If the upgrade requires the school to purchase new operating systems or equipment, the school may not be able to afford using the software.

ARE NEW EDITIONS COMING?

New editions are used by textbook companies to improve their products, but they also make more money on new editions than they do when booksellers sell their books used. States and districts fight the lure of a bright shiny new edition by restricting adopting textbooks to every so many years. But software is so new that rules may not apply. A school team will have to decide if a new edition of a product is worth the additional cost. For example, if a math program is purchased for the fourth grade, is the new edition truly a benefit to learning, or have they just added more dancing rabbits, speed, color, or whistles? Some tech people have asked electronic product developers to provide the same guarantee that textbook publishers do. That is, for the length of the adoption the company will agree to continue to produce that edition with the same system and computer requirements.

DO THE COMPUTERS HAVE TO BE NETWORKED?

For the Intranet

Intranet networking connects the school's computers together so they can be maintained from one central location. The largest benefit for technical staff is that they can sit in their offices and have access to computers all over the school. This greatly enhances their ability to respond quickly to software problems and cuts the cost of maintenance and reimaging since they don't have to travel to or sit in front of individual computers. The best scenario for technical staff is for all the computers to have the same operating system, software, plug-ins, and so on so they can standardize when they do reimaging or upgrading. Rather than having to remember that Ms. Jones needs a new browser edition, Mr. Smith needs a certain plug-in, and Ms. White uses a very old version of Flash, they can put the same technology on all computers. But this is not going to happen because, remember, schools cannot just throw away old computers in the trash. As new ones arrive, they come with new editions of operating systems, different software, and different amounts of memory and RAM. There still has to be some compromise in standardization so that tech staff can work effectively, but not so much compromise that it strangles innovation and creativity.

Teachers, support staff, and front office staff need to have their computers networked in order to report and exchange data. Some data could just be notices going to teachers or discussions among teachers in one discipline or grade. Information going over an intranet versus the Internet provides a bit more security for sensitive data. This makes the intranet also good for electronic classroom management software and the posting of grades.

For the Internet

The advantage of programs that are housed on the Internet is that the maintenance of the product is the responsibility of the publishing company or manufacturer. Chances are CDs, like floppy disks and external modems, will become a fond memory. With Internet programs, the school does not have to make space on a computer, fix broken links or errant pages, and ensure that it operates every day. But the school does have to maintain the Internet connection and the student computers. As more and more commercial products are accessed through the Internet, schools will have to prepare for the time when there are enough Internet connections to accommodate a majority of the school using the Internet every hour of the day.

Remember, early on it was thought that computers would just automatically be hooked up to the Internet because students were going to access free materials or wander around the Internet for information. However, as computers come more into use, automatic access to the Internet is no longer valid. Not all computers need to be networked. Designated or limited-use computers that are specialized for a program or a couple of programs don't need constant reimaging, upgrades, or technical support. For example, an elementary teacher could use old computers with an old word processing program as writing stations. It is too expensive to upgrade the computers and the students are only using them for supplemental or extracurricular activities. They are better left to die in peace.

SUMMARY

There are many decisions that business managers need to consider when purchasing computers. Making informed decisions as to what type of computers are needed and how they fit into the schools technology plan can save the school money and at the same time allow the school to retain more computers. The factors that need to be weighed are unique to each school and its goals and objectives for student progress. Business managers need to mediate between teachers and technical staff to ensure that whenever possible the purchases are made at the optimal time so that teachers can use them and staff can install and maintain them and that the computer that is purchased matches how it will be used.

Chapter Fourteen

Successful Classroom Models for Adapting Technology

Now, finally, what to do with classroom computers? In the period between early adopters and the early majority and the creation of a stable infrastructure there was a lot of experimentation going on. This was another stroke of luck in advancing technology integration because it permitted individual teachers to try out different types of electronic delivery in the classroom before any large purchases were made. The results show that there are many ways in which teachers can successfully and effectively integrate technology besides the model of one-computer, one-child. Their teaching goals are the guides for what type of technology, if any, they need to use.

None of the solutions that teachers found were of the one perfect classroom that educational researchers could scientifically announce, "Aha! (Point finger in air) Put computers in a circle/long row/cluster and this is the most optimal arrangement." The EL studies were in search of a pattern for how teachers could integrate technology or recipe for success and the pattern was no pattern, no easy bake recipe. But each teacher's solutions come as a result of their being in different types of facilities, socioeconomic area, ethnic mix, and theme schools. All the teachers incorporated computers into the curriculum differently. All of them were restricted to what they could do within the facilities the school provided. EL's success was to make the program as flexible to teachers so that they could pick and choose activities that fit their technology situation.

All of the above makes it complicated for business managers to manage technology. It would be so easy if technology integration into curriculum could be like a well oiled McDonald's kitchen assembly line. Kazillions of hamburgers made over the years all to taste and look identical. If an innovative machine, computer or process comes to light all the restaurants change.

The customer never knows the difference except he received the hamburgers two seconds earlier, they had less salt/fat/whatever, or they are .005 cents cheaper to produce. However students aren't like hamburgers and management and assessment of technology integration isn't like assessing the number of fries a worker spilled on the floor.

Business managers have to factor in a thousand different variables from a hundred different sources and determine how to apply it to thirty different types of classroom situations to make an informed decision that guarantees a high quality of learning experience for all students in the school. Winning at this is like winning the gold medal in the Mediators' Olympics. This exemplifies why business managers need to be actively involved in mediation to even out the playing field.

Remember the teacher with the illegal computers? She was an excellent model for how a creative and aggressive teacher can gain technology in her or his room. Her principal wisely closed his eyes and let her charge on in her own merry way. However she was also an example of how closing eyes in one situation could cause wide-eyed, scary problems for later. This perfect classroom was headed toward a big school-wide mediation meltdown and expose reasons that technology needs to be governed by a long term plan. Before discussing examples, this thought needs to be clarified. It is hard to say that the presence of technology means that that teacher is a better teacher. Teachers not using technology are good also. That being said, when one teacher offers technology options for students they learning field and opportunities are not equal for the students. Teachers with technology have more tools to offer opportunities that other teachers could not.

As an example for those of you who are not into the sciences Biology: Exploring Life came out at the bottom half of the genome project; it was a textbook rewriting event. So much new information was coming out that altered, corrected, and added to fundamental knowledge. For example Dolly, the cloned sheep, changed the belief that once a cell made a decision what it was going to be, it could not change that decision. However, Dolly changed all that. This discovery is one reason why the Genetic Science Learning Center was an instant hit and has continued to be such an important curriculum supplement; electronic curriculum can respond immediately. Print Textbooks and curriculum publishers could not keep up, but with EL's electronic materials it could and even on the spot. The teachers without technology were working with out of date print texts and having to create their own teaching materials if they wanted to show update the materials on their own.

Students in technology classrooms gain experience and practice to be more comfortable using computers as a teaching tool, understanding how to use interactives to increase learning, or at least the enjoyment of learning. Students were able to match their learning style with the teaching strategy of the materials. Like a game they could do interactives repetitively until they had the correct answers, practice putting chromosomes in the correct order, or reading the text materials. Of course some gained advanced skills on how to bypass filters to read email and MySpace and download amazing games. Through the Web Quests students were learning about what information was out there on the Internet that linked to science subjects and stretching out of the popular teenage sites.

Also students don't have to physically take home a textbook and the materials are accessible anywhere. Don't underestimate the difficulty students have lugging textbooks home. Publishing companies like to have a one-size-fits all curriculums textbook that is encyclopedic so no matter what the state standard teachers in New York and Kansas can have the materials they need. Students are very unhappy about hauling thirty pounds of textbooks around all day so, if they want to take them home, they have to strategize how they are going to hit the locker and not miss the bus, often an unsuccessful venture if gossip is good that day. Bullies take books away from nerds. But we are even assuming that the schools can afford to give each student a textbook to take home. A growing and alarming number of schools cannot. Electronic materials just need the Internet.

This model is an important one for how a teacher can economically gather enough equipment to have a rich array of technology. Although a low cost alternative for the teacher, it was a high cost alternative for the school. After a quick tour looking at other classrooms, it was noticed that most of the teachers from whom she had gotten the televisions did/could not replace them. She had an abundance of computers from the vocational classes, but she took most of them and other teachers did not have that resource. Her class was rich in technology but others were not. This was a repetitive pattern in most schools. There was often more of a technology gap between teachers in a school than there was between schools.

This is great for the students in that one teachers classroom until a parent or caretaker like you or me says, "Why isn't my student in that class? I want them transferred in." Parents and caretakers reading this book probably are quizzing their students right now if their teachers are providing them with electronic options. As stated before, no matter what types of socioeconomic school students attend there is no guarantee that all teachers are providing the same opportunities. This is where business managers have to step in and mediate to make sure that when an early adopter raises the teaching bar for the school, that he or she makes opportunities and creates incentives for the other teachers to also expand learning opportunities.

Another one of the teachers discussed was a model for how teachers can win grant money to purchase her own equipment and the principal continually reinforced her achievements by supplying more technology money. As the old equipment faded he helped replace them and if the grant did not quite afford all the equipment needed, he supplemented it. During the interview with him, he confirmed that the teachers in his school who used technology received more technology. This behavior and action turned out to be a common statement and action from principals, system managers, and district people. Teachers who used technology got technology.

This is great, with the exception that while he was rewarding one teacher with technology money while other teachers were not getting any technology. This seemed to be a common dilemma that occurred in schools, especially when there was pressure from many different stakeholders for schools to integrate technology before teachers were trained, infrastructures were inconsistent, and electronic materials were immature. It solved one problem, however it would be a safe bet that the Teachers' Lounge gossip hovers around why *some* teachers get more money and attention than *others*. But that is just one part of the situation that can arise in which the business manager needs to be a mediator.

Both teachers above also modeled another problem. At some time the technology staff was going to inherit all of the computers and the infrastructure. Even though the first teacher had found the lowest end computer to use for the EL program, eventually another upgrade would put her out of business. This was a pilot test, but had they purchased the program, they would have had a program and no computers. The second teacher had a growing mound of equipment, some of which may have been fixable or work with someone else's equipment. The business manager would have to mediate between the teacher and tech staff to determine the best route for these computers but most importantly, her successful grant writing skills should have been assisted by the tech staff to purchase equipment that would be compatible with the schools' overall goals.

Remember the students stuck in the doorway temporarily stopping the flow of traffic? Despite the difficulties of using labs, the teacher was successful making them a regular part of her routine by gaining the principal's support for priority scheduling. Problem one, the lounge was humming with why *some* teachers get special treatment when *others* do not.

There was another problem. The teacher had originally commandeered old computers that had been recycled out of an old computer lab and put them on her lab benches in the back of the room. The principal told her he would have the tech staff network the computers so she could use them. Now imagine the tech staff getting a work order in the middle of the school year to stop everything and hook up eight old computers in a room where they had to run cable around the room. Not that this was the complete problem, the Internet connection to the school was not large enough to handle daily traffic. Eight computers would have just added to the problem, slowing the system down even more. It is not hard to imagine tech staff receiving the order and thinking, "That's not going to happen."

However the good natured teacher, after four months of the computers sitting dead on her lab benches, found another combination of resources to meet her teaching goals. Through networking and searching the Internet, she found a company that sold electronic whiteboards and negotiated free use of the equipment in exchange for writing articles about her experience. She also found a grade book and quizzing software package that had been developed by a regional university. She used this equipment to give students practice for the state tests.

The teacher used the quizzing software as individual homework. The students were to answer a quiz and it was pretty tough. After they took the quiz, the software reported how many questions the students answered correctly and how many wrong. They could take the quiz as many times as they wanted until they got all the answers correct. In order to do this, the students had to revisit every question and confirm their answers. The quiz would lock up when the homework was due so it was a race for time to get all the questions correct. The exercise took on a game like quality when, in the computer lab, the students could work together to get all the answers.

The benefit to the school is that it gave them the opportunity to experiment with the equipment and to learn, from student data how that type of teaching technique affected student scores on achievement tests before they purchased the expensive equipment. This would give the business manager the evidence he or she needed to begin working with other teachers about using this type of technology or identifying the students who are improving or doing better than expected by using this teaching technique. And, of course, the equipment was a loaner for testing so eventually it will have to be paid for and tech staff will need to add it to their equipment to support; all additions on to the budget that the business manager would have to mediate.

Wireless networks solved the problem of stringing expensive cables. However an amusing precursor to the story of one teacher is that half of the laptops were registered with one wireless hub and the remaining were registered with another. This happened because the building was U-shaped. One hub was on one side of the u and the other on the other side of the U. The classroom was in the bottom center of the U and both signals came into the classroom but with weak reception. Not knowing which computers were registered with which hub, the students carried the laptops around like divining rods until they could pick up a signal.

The laptop computers were purchased through a grant that was to the school although a single teacher wrote the grant on her on initiative. When the laptops arrived to the school, they were rightly issued to the library where the media center was and the teacher checked them out and put them in her classroom. This trick worked for a while until other enterprising teachers realized that those were school laptops not *her* laptops. This made interesting mediations.

Although the technology integration has been fragmented and seemingly a bit disorganized, these experiments have set the stage for a successful wide adoption of technology. As with any experiment, what works and doesn't work is revealed. The information is catalogued and the process starts again. This will continue. The idea of a perfect environment doesn't even meet with learning theory. Students learn differently, teachers teach differently, and subject areas require different types of skill development and sequential knowledge acquisition. New technologies will come rolling in, school buildings will get older, and new equipment will become old and fail. These dynamics will keep the search for the successful learning environment new, fresh, and focused on learners.

Another values of information technology is that years ago, if a teacher or business manager wanted to know what worked, they had to wait for a journal article to come out. No one is going to debate the value of refereed articles; however, add the time it takes to publish and most of the news is old. Electronic journals, news services, and Web sites that describe programs are all invaluable tools for accessing information about what works. When teachers do successful experiments on adapting facilities, the school Web site is also an excellent venue for broadcasting this to parents, colleagues, and potential funders. All of this adds up to the collective knowledge of how to create a successful learning environment.

SUMMARY

Two lessons were learned here for business managers who are ready for large integration of electronic materials and opportunities for students. One is that business managers will not have simple solutions to simple challenges. Early on the goal was to get some, any, technology in the school. It resulted in a digital divide within classrooms in a single school. This situation may not every be solved, but it could be better. The goal now is to provide all students with the equal opportunity to use electronic materials and tools. In order to do this business managers will have to look at long term goals and bring in all the teachers and tech staff to work in one common direction. But along with the school, business managers also have to express to publishers and software developers that they also need to consider how programs can accommodate the differences teachers have in facilities and abilities. That will never change. Electronic materials and make programs need to be flexible enough to adjust to varying situations.

The second is that experimentation with different types of technology and electronic materials is great, but only if it is followed by reflection of what has happened and how problems can be solved or avoided. Many teachers and schools have flown through innovative ideas and change without reporting them. These experimentations need to be followed with evaluation, reflection, and permanent reporting. Business managers can this facilitate by just asking at the time teachers or technology want to purchase whatever, "What evidence do you have that this will improve learning?"

Chapter Fifteen

What Electronic Materials Need to Be

Like the experiments teachers have done with learning environments, a lot of experiments using electronic materials need to be revisited and remeasured with rewritten research questions. Most studies were based on the assumption that technology-delivered curriculum would be a silver bullet that would benefit all students. Much of the testing was centered on whether or not computers were better than textbooks. That was the wrong question. The right question is how technology can increase the learning success of differentiated learners, students who have very different learning preferences and backgrounds. What is technology going to do for the student with a D or C average?

The intent of integrating electronic materials is not to put print textbooks out to pasture but to blend them with interactive and diverse electronic materials and activities. Not all students learn by reading a textbook. That is why electronic textbooks failed to catch on. Putting a textbook online is just a textbook in fuzzy print, and it doesn't change the teaching or learning style or technique. Technology still does not make text-rich documents appealing to the majority of learners, even with the sizeable cost savings and a sparkling-new appearance without other students' romantic artwork and graffiti. Copying print media into an electronic format does not take advantage of the diversity that technology offers, including visuals, audio, and interactives.

Think of electronic curriculum as a museum exhibit rather than a textbook. It is interactive, enticing the visitor into doing some action in order to learn, there is choice of where to enter and how to proceed, and clever navigation steers visitors toward the same learning goals while still making them feel as if they choose the path. There are many different techniques to deliver the message. Visitors can look at objects, push and pull an interactive component, watch something move, listen to an explanation, and even read. The physical environment changes from one area to the next to speed up or slow down visitors, to create a mood, and to highlight key concepts. Qualities that were once unique and restricted to a museum experience can be incorporated into the classroom using technology.

In the early days, museums' missions were to display objects, thousands of things. Two-headed sheep, arrowheads, shrunken heads, dressed fleas, stuffed bears, and half-unwrapped mummies were crammed into glass displays or clung on the walls just out of the reach of sticky-fingered kids. Visits to these museums mostly happened when the grandchildren visited grandma who, desperate to entertain but also desperate to protect her house, dragged them out. Feeling the pressure of the high cost of preserving these collections, museums took the two-headed goats off the floor, put them into the collections, and began building interactive exhibits that visitors could push, pull, and smack. This worked, and in the 1980s museums experienced huge pop cultural popularity, attracting unprecedented herds of visitors and, along with them, lots of federal and private funding. It was the dot-com era for museums, full of excitement and innovation. The popularity was attributed to the transformation from Don't Touch to Touch Me, interactive exhibits, and huge traveling blockbusters like King Tut and the Dinamation robotic dinosaurs.

This educational experience was called *edutainment*, a coinage that branded museums with a light and fluffy reputation with academics but endeared them to the general public. Contrary to criticisms, museums found that when they interviewed exiting visitors who just meaninglessly banged around exhibits without feeling they learned something new, the visitors left unhappy. They came to learn. If they had just wanted to be entertained, they could have played miniature golf. Behind the scenes, museum-exhibit designers and educators began the process of developing carefully orchestrated exhibits to attract and engage visitors in a meaningful learning experience. The research was conducted by exhibit designers, educators, and behavioral scientists, people who were intrigued by the visitors' reports that they learned a lot despite the observations of visitors running from exhibit to exhibit. The researchers wanted to know just how much visitors learned, what they learned, and how they could maneuver them into learning more.

They gave birth to the science of visitor studies. The Visitor Studies Association was organized for exhibit designers, educators, visitor-services staff, and marketers to exchange information and findings. Informal educators had an advantage that schools did not have: they could establish a new discipline of informal learning that had no baggage.

Because electronic curricula and lessons have many of the same powerful learning characteristics and attributes of a museum exhibit, the research methods, techniques, and measurement instruments these researchers used can be directly applied to developing and evaluating effective programs. This is not a benefit to be taken lightly. Museum visits are usually a one-shot but powerful educational deal: a grand, memorable, and highly charged shot, but one shot. That being said, these exhibits can do more to push a student toward a career path or encourage lifelong learning than does their schoolwork. Visitors are charged and vow to return and to learn more, but they go to the gift shop, make their purchases, and don't return until the next blockbuster traveling exhibit. By using electronic curriculum, schools can capture and sustain for everyday learning the same type of rich interactive experience that museums provide just once in a while.

This chapter is not intended to suggest that electronic curriculum should even remotely hint to students that learning or schoolwork is one big honkin' pile of fun. It ain't. Neither should electronic material be designed to constantly entertain, bribe, or cajole students into learning. A bit of that is nice, but, when students graduate and get jobs their bosses are not going to dream up fun ways to get them to produce a financial report in on time, frolic while tearing out an old toilet tank, or revel and stand smiling in front of an irate screaming customer whose plane was canceled because the snow on the runway was too deep and unsafe for the plane to take off. This chapter is saying that D and C students who are hampered by some challenge need to have more tools for learning than just reading and answering the questions in the back of the book. It also reinforces the idea that lots can be learned from research results found in informal education and that the results can be applied to exemplary electronic materials.

ELECTRONIC CURRICULUM SHOULD HAVE A NAVIGATION THAT ALLOWS STUDENTS TO USE MATERIALS AT THEIR COMFORT OR INTEREST LEVEL

When a group of visitors enters an exhibit, despite the fact they come as a social group, they spread out. Watch a mom try to reign in her kids as they sprint and dive toward an exhibit, bounding in different directions. Although where they go seems random, it is not. They usually choose something that builds on previous knowledge or emotion, and this spirits their motivation for learning. What attracted them could be an object that is familiar and favorite—a color, a texture, movement, or subject content. Whatever the reason, they decide that particular spot is where they want to start. They are interested, and they are self-motivated to investigate further. Mom will see them again at the gift store.

Electronic materials have the same power to let students choose to enter a program where they want to start. Their choices all cover the same content— let's say cells—but present it in a different manner: a video of real cells dividing, a game on naming the cell parts, or a cartoon of a cell taking in oxygen and spitting out carbon dioxide. Students could even read something. But whatever the students choose, it is because it fits their comfort level of understanding, preference for visual presentation, or reading level. They decided and they are engaged. The intent is to have them start where they feel comfortable and lead them smiling into more challenging materials and more depth of content.

Electronic materials should also give teachers choices of the materials that are most appropriate for the learning situation. Classroom dynamics are fascinating but challenging for the teacher. In one day there can be five sections of American history, and the mix of students in each section creates its own personality and atmosphere. Teachers can then pick and choose activities: an interactive timeline, video, or recording to match the make-up of the class demographics and academic level. For example, a teacher may want to mix active discussion with electronic video and audio activities to pick up the pace during the last class of the day. For a core class, the teacher may start with basic concepts, activities that reinforce, and then practice vocabulary and processes; for an honors class, the teacher may begin with more complex activities that require more critical thinking, using vocabulary and processes the students already know.

ELECTRONIC CURRICULUM SHOULD USE NOVELTY TO LEAD LEARNERS TO KEY CONCEPTS, NOT ENTERTAIN MINDLESSLY OR BE DISTRACTING

Visitors having choice and viewing exhibits as things catch their attention works well as a motivator. That is fine when the exhibit is displaying objects here and there. However, exhibit designers learned that if they want to tell a story or to teach a difficult concept that requires understanding this before understanding that, they could not have visitors wandering haphazardly around the exhibit. They needed to find a way to sequentially or logically lead the visitor. They solved this by enticing visitors to choose a common starting point by using something new, unexpected, or stimulating—something that was novel and that stood out or demanded attention. This same technique can be used to direct and guide students who are using electronic lessons.

Internet advertisers use novelty regularly with those annoying dancing shadows, shooting galleries, and flashing whatevers. Like it or not, the eye is attracted, and enough people click on the advertising gimmick to make it successful. Anyone who has ever been so annoyed that they left a Web page because the novelty was too distracting instinctively demonstrates the same thing that museum researchers found. Novelty misused or overused can become so much of a distraction that visitors become annoyed, frustrated, or confused and leave the environment. This was probably the reason for disillusionment with many of the early electronic materials, which hid poor content and frustrated people trying to find the information they wanted. They couldn't find it because of bouncing rabbits, overstimulating color, or interactive activities with little learning purpose. Novelty does not replace or hide bad materials that have poor and invalid content, poor navigation, or no instructional design plan.

Electronic materials should strategically use novelty as a technique to take students from their chosen activity, which was at their comfort level, and to prepare them to continue on to more challenging materials or bring them back to the conceptual starting point. Well-planned navigational design is essential for taking the students back and forth through the material. They may start with an activity, such as putting a cell together, but navigation leads them back to the place that explains why the hamburger-shaped thing manufactures protein and the bug-looking thing produces the power for the hamburger-shaped thing to run. This is something that museums cannot do. Once visitors have committed to a walking direction and have rushed past the cell parts, getting them to turn back through the exhibit when they are confused by why DNA is coming out of a hamburger thing is almost impossible. And if they do have to backtrack, it thoroughly annoys them. Walking through museums is linear; electronic materials are not.

ELECTRONIC MATERIALS SHOULD PREPARE STUDENTS TO LEARN WHAT THE TEACHERS INTENDED TO TEACH

Exhibit designers were frustrated because visitors were not zooming in on what they wanted to teach them. Some visitors went through an exhibit on Native Americans and learned that this people used predominately red, their favorite color, for artwork and clothes. Others learned that they used grasses and reeds, a rather strange-looking option, for clothes instead of what everyone thinks Indians used, leather. The exhibit-learning goal may have been to teach how the native people of the area adapted to the available natural resources. The funders want the museum to prove to them that that is what the visitors learned. In search of a solution, exhibit designers found that they could give visitors an advance organizer activity to focus visitor attention on the exhibit learning goals without distracting them from their own personal learning goals.

For example, going into an exhibit the visitor may find a computer or worksheet saying "Test Your Knowledge." One question might be, "What natural material did the native people who lived in and around Seattle use for clothing?" The options could be expected, leather; unexpected, grasses and reeds; and other options could be so wrong the visitor could guess, like polyester, or harder to guess, like cotton. Or the advance organizer could be to match the natural materials different Indian groups used to make clothing. The choices could be grasses and reeds, feathers, milkweed, and leather listed next to Plains Indians, Mesoamericans, Ohio Valley Indians, and Pacific Coast Indians. After visitors take the test, they are curious to find the answers, and they search the exhibits to discover whether they were right or not.

Teachers have used quizzes as advance organizers in the schools, but grading or responding to them immediately and doing them frequently has always been problematic. Remember, high-school teachers have between one hundred and two hundred students a day. Electronic curriculum can deliver a quick quiz or a fast question and quickly draw students' attention to looking for the answer. The multiple choice question can be shown on the whiteboard and, after contemplating the answer as an individual or as a group, a student can use the clicker to vote their answer. When the correct answer is shown, the students can immediately check their response and then can reflect on their understanding. If the results of the student responses are sent to the teacher and then put on a graph, the teacher can quickly glance to check if the material is in the students' comfort range and which students might need individual attention to bring them up to speed.

ELECTRONIC MATERIALS SHOULD USE QUESTIONING OR CHALLENGING STATEMENTS TO ENCOURAGE STUDENTS TO QUESTION WHAT THEY THOUGHT THEY KNEW

Museums use questions and statements that challenge visitors' previous understanding or preconceptions of how things happen or work. For example, a sign in large print that can be read far from the exhibit reads, "Which Is the Blood-Sucking Bat?" When visitors look into the case, they see different types of bats and what they eat. They learn that, contrary to Hollywood's image of bats, most bats do not live on blood and those that do do not prefer the blood of baseball-bat-swinging humans. If the sign read "Bat Species of the World," it would not get anyone charged up or curious.

ELECTRONIC CURRICULUM SHOULD USE VISUALS, INTERACTIVES, AND AUDIO TO EXPLAIN CONCEPTS WHEN STUDENTS CHOOSE NOT TO READ, PREFER NOT TO READ, OR CANNOT READ

Informal educators never fell for the misconception that smart people have an incredible love of reading. They learned this by watching visitors as they went through exhibits with hardly a glance and wandered past exhibits with too much or too-difficult text. When the Cincinnati Museum of Natural History and Science, on the cusp of the museum boom, was preparing to move to their new home in Union Terminal, they did extensive pilot testing of the new exhibit labels. They accomplished this by putting paper, marker marked, and tape exhibits and label text on the old museum floor. As visitors went through, a researcher asked them to look at the artifacts, interactive, or design and the accompanying text. They would read and relay what they understood. Keep in mind that over 40 percent of the museum members had a college degree plus some graduate credits and, in general, museum visitors have a higher education level than groups at other public events. This being said, the testing showed that labels had to be at no more than a sixth-grade reading level. Visitors wanted the information quick to read, easy to understand, and to the point. It's the same thing writing teachers need a rubber stamp for: "What are you trying to tell me?"

The second misconception is that if smart people have a high reading level in their profession or a particular interest, they will have the same level in other disciplines. A doctor, lawyer, physicist, or accountant cannot naturally understand the terminology used by people who are trained and educated in the natural sciences. For example, geneticists say DNA is amplified during replication. Great. To many, this means that DNA is louder. Isn't music louder with amplifiers? Each science has created a language of words that have a specific meaning, a meaning that doesn't always match how a word is commonly used in everyday conversation. Accountants know what absorbed costs are. Physicists know what absolute uncertainty is. Writers know what homophones are. No one else does. The important point here is that not understanding jargon does not reflect a person's intelligence or ability to succeed. It is more a sign of the ability of an author to relate the subject matter to those who are not in the same field. Why would students be any different from museum members? There are more museum members than scientists. Not being able to read fast or at an advanced level doesn't always mean that a student cannot understand complicated science, math, humanities, and behavioral concepts. There are many reasons that students may not be able to or want to read. That center of the brain may not be functioning well; English may not be their primary language; they may be dyslexic; they may not have had the opportunity to read at an early age; they may have a home life that is too disruptive; they may not be able to take textbooks home. The reasons goes on. This is the essence of electronic curriculum and lessons: the interactives, video, audio, and use of graphics deliver tools to students who are not speed-readers or even good readers so they can understand the basic principles of something or understand abstract thoughts or processes. Students may not be able to comprehend from text or a dramatic illustration how DNA makes copies of itself, but they can understand by watching a video, manipulating an animated interactive depicting the steps, or listening to a description. There will be many more people talking about reports and comments about this book than actually reading it.

ELECTRONIC CURRICULUM SHOULD LAYER WRITTEN INFORMATION IN BITE-SIZED CHUNKS THAT PROGRESSIVELY LEAD THEM INTO MORE DETAIL

Museum researchers found that visitors don't want to encounter lots of text. They want to decide early on if they are interested before they commit to spending time when there are so many choices. Exhibits will draw visitors in by presenting a subject, then ask them to do something to read more. News sites do this well by giving a picture and some text that gives just enough information so that, if interested, the viewer can click. If the visitor is not interested, there is an immediate list of other topics. When the visitor does click, more choices await embedded in the article or at the side with suggestions of other articles, slide shows, and videos. Exhibits only have a couple of seconds to convince a visitor to make a commitment to stay. Acres of text appear to be too long a commitment. Designers found if they only exposed a small amount of text at a time, they could tease visitors to make an action, lift a panel, push a button, or whatever to get to the second layer of text. If the visitors are still interested, they will continue until they have, without realizing it, read an acre of text. Had they seen what they were going to read from the start, they would have just meandered past.

It is common to see students open a textbook, look at the commitment involved, deeply sigh, roll their eyes back, drop their shoulders, and sink despairingly down into the seat. Electronic curriculum can solve that behavior by using the same techniques exhibits do. It can layer text so that students only see a portion at a time. This not only entices students into reading, it allows them time to reflect and digest concepts as they continue on deeper into the layers. Scrolling doesn't count as layering. Watch students as they get on a Web site and scroll down to see how much they are going to have to read. They will deeply sigh, roll their eyes back, drop their shoulders, and click onto something else. Scrolling has the same effect as starting to read chapter 1 of a seven-hundred-page textbook.

Exemplary electronic materials need to use layering in their visual and navigational design. The layering can be accomplished in many ways through clever navigation. Information can be given in the form of slide shows, taking an old technique and modernizing it by adding text or audio to narrate. It can be given as pop-ups on a map of the Oregon Trail, narrating the difficulties pioneers had trekking across the plains, hiking up the mountains, and battling cold and hot, dry and wet. Another example is a simple activity like a written math problem, which might start with obvious things to multiply and divide. Additional problems become increasingly tricky and rigorous as students learn to weed out information and determine what they actually need to use to solve the problem. Whatever the method, the text needs to be presented in bite-size chunks. As students progress into the concept, the text can get longer and longer.

ELECTRONIC MATERIALS SHOULD HAVE INTERACTIVES THAT USE EFFECTIVE LEARNING TECHNIQUES

Visitors know there will be exhibits that have interactives, and they will look for these first. The design of the interactives is important to the overall success of the exhibit in fostering learning. They may be the reason people come to the museum, but they are not the reason they return; interactives are the sizzle, not the steak, and people cannot live on sizzle. Exhibit designers know from experience that interactives must be simple to use and quick to figure out and that when visitors encounter them something must happen right then and there. One exhibit that was observed had the controls in one part of the exhibit, but the action occurred in another area just about six inches to the left; the person working the controls had to turn his or her head to watch the action. Because the visitors were expecting the action to happen directly in front of them, they soon tired and walked on, ignoring the directions to look to the left. The action they created was blinded by a more novel exhibit further to the right. They assumed that the one they were using was broken and the other, blinking one might work.

Most visitors approach an interactive, immediately begin poking and prodding to start it going, make an observation, then look around for an explanation. They are annoyed if there are obstacles in their way. This same behavior was observed in students when they log on to a Web site. This is where the authors and developers of materials, who love to write and read, abruptly bump into those who want to do, question, and then, finally, read. Creating an interactive is a skilled science and depends on the goal that it is designed to achieve. Some interactives in museums are specifically designed to draw visitors into wanting to learn more. They present a situation that discomforts the knowledge of the visitor. How can it do that? Why did that happen? This is neat; what is this? Others take the place of reading. Museum researchers know that interactives are shorthand for learning: visitors like them, and visitors learn.

Interactive activities in electronic curriculum have to play by the same rules that museums have learned through extensive research on exhibits. The first is that the interactive has to deliver the information the students need to know, but at the same time the program has to use sound educational and behavioral techniques to draw them in. Visitors come to the museum knowing they will be able to interact with the exhibits. Without this interactive quality, museums would still be the get-out-of-the-house event during the visit with grandma. The other rule museums have learned is that the interactives cannot stand alone as just something fun to do. They must be tools for learning, either to draw visitors in or to reach visitors who have the intelligence but prefer not to read long, jargon-laden text.

ELECTRONIC MATERIALS SHOULD BE OPEN HOLIDAYS AND WEEKENDS

Museums do much of their business on Saturdays and Sundays, but some of the largest moneymaker activities for museums are the evening and after-hours events. The most annoying thing about going to a museum is discovering that the targeted exhibit is shut down for a special event that evening. People spend a ton of money to rent museums for dinners, cocktails, lectures, bar mitzvahs, weddings, and so on. There are literally hundreds of thousands of Girl Scouts, Boy Scouts, church groups, and other youth organizations that spend a night at the museum. The point is that learning is not a 9 a.m.–to–4 p.m. activity; neither is teaching. Students need to be able to access materials to read or activities to do when they are ready—usually, to their social distress, on Friday night. They need to be able to access electronic materials when teachers do not use them. This equalizes the playing field. Teachers need to be able to prepare for classes during their planning time, which usually means Sunday afternoon at 3:00.

ELECTRONIC MATERIALS SHOULD BE EASY FOR TEACHERS TO USE SO THEY HAVE MORE TIME TO SPEND WITH STUDENTS

Teachers have limited time to devote to developing materials. To outsiders, it seems as if teachers have all the time in the world—hours shorter than a banker's, many holidays, and an extended break during summer. But there is another way to look at this, and that can be delicate to explain. This subject is explosive. Teaching is low-paid, considering the advanced level of education teachers earn. It is not always thought of as a prestigious and certainly not a lucrative profession. The United States needs to recruit thousands of new teachers every year with the job advertisement of hard work, low prestige, average pay, and no merit increase in salary. One benefit that is attractive is the extra time teachers can spend with their family and on other interests. Another benefit is that teachers like to be with and work with students. Their other interests often include students, for example, being a band director, coaching a team, being a newspaper advisor, organizing the art club, advising student council, tutoring struggling students, and so on. They are very, very busy people in and out of school.

The popularity of textbooks has been in part attributed to the fact that they offer a neat and tidy curriculum, which often dictates what will be taught if the teacher is not comfortable in the subject matter. Elementary teachers don't take college courses in all the subjects they have to teach. In some subjects, they may have taken only one course in a topic like European history during the Middle Ages. Even high-school teachers who majored in a subject may not have taken many, if any, higher-level courses. High-school teachers may be teaching out of field or be teaching a subject that they majored in twenty years ago, while the textbook is ten years old. It is difficult to expect teachers to excel without supportive materials that are continually updated as new information, ideas, or discoveries become known.

Electronic materials must be able to support teachers with current, valid, and accurate information written by content experts that is easy to transform to the classroom. Teachers don't have time to wade though a hundred Web sites, gather, or rewrite materials for this chapter and then that chapter. They cannot be expected to spend seven hours a day in class, be responsible for one hundred or more students, be the advisor for a club, and keep absolutely current with the latest innovations in their field. The same characteristics that interest visitors and students in learning can be applied to making it easy for teachers to keep updated on materials, pose questions, and pick and choose the appropriate materials for students with just a click.

ELECTRONIC MATERIALS SHOULD
BE UNDER ONGOING EVALUATION

Materials should include diagnostic methods to help the teacher to evaluate the progress of the students as they continue through the material. These evaluations should be easy for the teacher to analyze. For example, there are some types of activities, such as a check-your-knowledge quiz, a task to perform, or a product that students have to produce, that show they understand the process or concept they have been taught. This information can be used by the teacher to either step up the class or to circle around and backtrack to materials that were not well understood. The assessments should be student specific so the teacher can determine which students might be out of step with the rest of the class and so he or she can plan appropriate activities or actions for those learning too slowly or too quickly. Finally, the assessments must be built-in and easy for the teacher to use.

SUMMARY

Electronic materials should use all the advantages of technology to deliver curriculum and materials that employ a wide variety of teaching methods and techniques. The students and teachers should have a choice in how they learn materials: via audio, visual, interactives, or reading. Novelty and other ways to gain students' attention should be used effectively to engage students, not distract them from learning. Navigation should be well crafted to lead students through materials easily even if they do not start at the same point. The materials should be easy for teachers to tailor for the age, interest, and scholastic ability of the students in different classrooms.

Materials should be evaluated according to whether they have local solutions to local problems. Do they address the teaching goals? Are the materials flexible enough to target a specific challenge a school has? If teachers use a program to increase reading skills for students who are slightly under the state standard reading level, does the program increase their motivation to read more, their comprehension of what they read, and their vocabulary? If teachers choose a program to increase math skills, does the program give students practice and immediate reinforcement and then automatically lead them on to more difficult concepts as they reach certain levels of understanding?

Chapter Sixteen

The Leadership Role
of Business Managers

The business managers are the central figures in watching over, managing, and mediating how the school will acquire and use technology as well as provide professional support, training, and development. This entails a lot of mediation and remediation in the four areas that rely on technology: the central office, shared labs, the library, and classrooms. The first step is to conduct strategic planning for both the short-term, the next two to three years, and the long-term, the next five to ten years, to organize the creation of a governance plan with representatives from each area. The second step is to establish management policies and procedures for efficient daily operation in purchasing, computer repair and maintenance, and system operations, including Internet and intranet. This is the business end: putting in place a successful technology infrastructure that will serve the computers and other technology to meet or exceed the school's learning goals, facilities, and budget.

Business managers are also the central figures in leading teachers and support staff to leverage educational purchasing power to establish a gold standard of quality and buying policies for software, operating systems, and hardware. Schools need to evaluate how they are going to use electronic materials, when they will use them, and who will use them. To do this, business managers, teachers, and staff need statistics that give an account of where their students are and what types of learning strategies they need to use in order to improve their students' interest, knowledge, and skills. This also means knowing when a teacher, subject, or treatment for students doesn't need an electronic program.

TECHNOLOGY INFRASTRUCTURE

The best qualifications for technical staff are affected by multilayered factors, because each school has a distinctly different quality, quantity, and level of technical resources provided by the district and state. This makes a big difference in the required or preferred background training and abilities of the tech staff when new hires or appointments are made. For example, some schools have little tech support from the district and have to go it alone. This could be because the district is small or badly funded or the school may be so large that it is a tech industry within itself and needs a large, highly technical staff, regardless of what the district provides. If the district maintains the computers, provides the network, and has a strong technical staff, the business manager might determine that the best hire for the school would be a repairperson to give immediate support for computer maintenance. However, the learning goals of the school also have to be considered. Rather than a repairperson, the teachers may need an instructional designer to assist them in creating or using materials and management tools specific to the learning challenge. Business managers will have to work with the school and district to assess the best hire.

Another factor that enters into decision making is knowing when to push and politic for appropriate, deserved, and better services. An example is the school that had an Internet capacity that was larger than what the district's pipe supplied. When the school hit its peak hours at 9:15 a.m., the Internet connection bogged down. Unfortunately, peak hours continued until the end of the school day at 3:15 p.m. This does not suggest that the school should restrict its purchases to the lowest common denominator; it does suggest that the business manager needs to conduct some strategic politicking and public relations to negotiate with the district or other stakeholders to supply the school with the technology they need to get the job done. Stakeholder funds can be swayed by logical, well-presented, and effective arguments that show how their money is an investment in the future of the students in their community, voting district, or area of business.

One of the most important actions that business managers will have to take is working with technical staff from the schools, districts, and states to start the process of stabilizing technology infrastructure. This will entail establishing guidelines for companies to follow in producing products that guarantee a high degree of reliability, establish a tolerance level for upgrades, and standardize product compatibility. Schools need to invest more in integration of technology into the curriculum and therefore need to invest their money into learning programs for students, not constantly waste money updating hardware and software just to keep word-processing applications going.

CENTRAL OFFICE

Collecting data that shows the progress students and schools make is important for teachers in assessing and deciding what teaching strategies are needed in the school, a level, or class. States and districts usually have set information they require schools to collect; however, business managers must still have an eye out for what data the school needs for its own use. This information is essential not only for assessment but for schools and individual teachers who, short of regular funds, are writing grants to achieve their specific learning goals. At the end of projects, this information will be valuable for use on evaluation reports that show funders what their money helped the school to achieve. This data can mean the difference between being successful in winning the next grant or not.

When collecting student and school data, business managers will be charged with the security, ethical, and legal issues that come along with holding sensitive data. Schools, districts, states, and the federal government have never had so much potential for using quantitative data to improve education by making schools accountable to their students and stakeholders. That being said, collecting private data also raises new questions about the confidentiality of this information and when or if it becomes invasive. Business managers will also be charged with keeping the information secure from those who have criminal intent or those who are just hacking to improve their grades. Policies and procedures for collecting and securing data need to be established both locally and nationally. This is not just for the computers but also for the people who might legitimately have access.

The central office is the center for electronic communication that projects the school's visual identity and academic quality, which frames the community's perception and expectations of the school. This communication will often determine how stakeholders will interact with and participate in the school's or individual teachers' initiatives. Electronic communications can be used proactively to promote the school, keep stakeholders who may be potential funders aware of the successes and achievements of the school, and build its reputation for exemplary educational efforts. This is also the central location for parents and caregivers to connect with and work with the school, to keep their students on track, and to become actively involved as volunteers and resources.

LIBRARY

The library is probably one of the more interesting areas in which to plan change. Libraries will more closely integrate information management into the curriculum as well as provide traditional library services. This change will be in two areas. One is the cultivation of electronic resources like e-books or other reading materials that students can access or download from school, home, or wherever they may be to whatever computer or auxiliary equipment they have. The technology may not be there yet for text-laden materials to have the same visual appeal as other materials; however, it is better to have this option and to get ready for it, since the technology is just around the corner. A mixture of paper books and electronic books gives students more options for ways they can access materials. That is the essence of technology: making materials fairer and more available for more students.

The other area of change is that students are going to be entering an information-rich work environment that needs to be controlled by the user through skilled and informed search strategies, critical thinking, and assessment of the validity of the information the user finds on the Internet. Students will need to be able to research information and write or present a logical argument to a posed problem. For example, students learn about meiosis, how the mom's egg and the dad's sperm interact to make a baby, but can they evaluate the quality and soundness of information they find on the Internet about inherited diseases or the results of a DNA paternity test? Working together, librarians and teachers can use instructional design techniques to blend research strategies, assessment of materials, and information management with traditional courses.

It is also important for teachers and support staff to access the library databases in order to continue their professional development and increase their knowledge about teaching and supporting students. Diverse learners also means diverse students with many challenges; therefore, teachers and support staff have to be constant problem solvers and also keep aware of new issues. For example, a school may suddenly have thirty new ESL (English as a Second Language) students appear, and the teachers must learn about their language, culture, and religion to devise a program to integrate them into the rest of the student body. A teacher may have to research information to help a student with a particular learning disability or unusual behavior.

Because of the diverse skills, education, and backgrounds of librarians, business managers will want to thoughtfully consider the qualifications of the people hired to work in the library in order to complement the needs of all departments. People with an instructional design background in technology are orphans, belonging neither completely in the technological nor the educational spheres. If the business manager takes a little from each budget and adds it to the library, an instructional designer could be added to the library staff to purposefully intertwine teaching, information management, and technology.

STAKEHOLDERS

Stakeholders, those that create policity and those who provide money, are like teenagers: they need to date, flirt, and hold hands, and you cannot let them out of your sight for a minute. Control comes from knowing they are there and being proactive, not reactive. Technology helps that. With one click, school newsletters, press releases, and other brag documents can be broadcast to legislators, potential donors, and businesses to keep the flirtation going. And most organizations have newsletters, e-mail alerts, and other communications that schools can tap into to keep aware of what they are doing. Government and private organizations that have money to give also provide electronic newsletters that list the grant offerings, news about philanthropy, and so on to schools.

Stakeholders who are funders are just as anxious to connect with exemplary schools as schools are to connect with them. Technology has made it much easier for schools to learn about funding sources, what they want to fund, and the process of making a winning grant proposal. It behooves funders to broadcast their grants in order to attract as many proposals from a wide variety of schools from different demographic, geographic, and socioeconomic areas. For example, the Department of Education has a host of electronic services that permit the user to search for grants by what is coming up next, by program, by theme, and so on. They also provide access to abstracts and descriptions of present and previously funded grants so schools can learn what types of grants have been funded and how they fared. This is important information for learning what types of projects the funder prefers and what the successes and challenges were for similar grants.

STUDENTS

Listen to the students. That is a clear message that technology professionals repeat over and over again. Educational marketing is an interesting animal because it often results in a product that is produced for and marketed to the buyers and not to the users. For example, publishers will do focus groups and extensive analysis to learn the characteristics and features teachers or textbook committees will consider for a purchase. The product is always within the committee's comfort zone. This was a problem during the early years of the adoption of technology. Schools were just gearing up to use computers and pondering whether that Internet thing was going to catch on while students were already banging away at anything that was electronic and could get to the Internet.

Students want wide and extended access to materials and technology. Business managers need to provide them with programs that they can access 24/7, because, for reasons other than their personal commitment to learning, students don't always have the time or energy for learning during school hours. It is only fair to expect that students are very much like adults: they can't always be expected to react when others expect them to. They have sports, hobbies, civic engagements, personal trauma, work, bad days, girlfriend or boyfriend troubles, challenges with time management, and so on. Sometimes they need more time to read, view, or listen in order to comprehend a subject. Business managers also need to partner with school facilities or public libraries, community centers, and other nontraditional sources to provide before- and after-school access to computers. This access is an important resource for students who do not have computers at home, have too much competition with other family members, or have out-of-date computers.

Business managers need to work with teachers and staff to use technology to present materials using various teaching techniques to connect to the various learning styles of students when textbooks and hands-on activities, for whatever reason, do not fit the bill. Students' learning preferences are influenced by many things and are constantly changing. For example, students live in a digital environment that provides them with a barrage of visuals, music, and rapid-fire responses that adults were not raised with. They do not know life without electronics. Like it or not, this environment has led to students responding to stimulus and learning situations in different ways, and this will be the world in which they will find employment. However, students have to also learn the difference between a picture of the Grand Canyon and the feel of hanging over the edge of the observation deck. They need to see DNA come from something they eat, like strawberries, and tease out and pull the muscles of a supermarket chicken wing to learn how birds fly.

Technology also helps students keep connected to school. There are thousands of reasons students become lost in life: caregivers move, migrate, and change, and students leave their caregivers, get suspended from school, go skiing, have accidents, get sick, and so on. Students can sometimes overcome the circumstances that keep them away when they are able to gain access to the Internet and when they can continue on with their schooling from wherever they are or in any circumstances.

TEACHERS

Early adopters will always be the leadership to change and chaos. They will stretch the system and find whatever is new: good, bad, or ugly. Business managers need to cheer them on and encourage them to find money and resources on one hand but on the other hand keep them from getting into too much trouble. In many ways, it is lucky that they are only a small percentage of teachers. If what they are doing is good and applicable to what other teachers can do to improve learning in their classroom, the early majority will follow. That is where business managers have to pay close attention, because this new group of adopters represents the bulk of teachers, is expensive, and will require much more management, money, and attention. As they refine the teaching techniques and apply them to general classroom practices, this group will be the sustaining factor that changes a glitzy trend into a solid and established teaching practice.

Not all teachers are going to use technology. There are numerous reasons, too many to list here, but the bottom line is that some teachers simply won't use it. They don't like it, they don't learn well using technology, and it is not a teaching technique that they enjoy, have patience for, or are skilled at using. The difference between how many teachers use technology within a school is as big as the difference in the use of technology among schools. That will improve as technology becomes more common in classrooms, but what will not change is that teachers will use technology differently or not at all. Again, this does not mean sinking to the lowest common denominator. If one biology teacher out of four doesn't like to use computers, that alone is not a reason to forego a purchase of an electronic program that the rest of the teachers will use. What it does mean is that teachers need to look for a program that students can access on their own and that is not limited to school hours. That is the great equalizer.

Classroom management software accomplishes many things for the school. First, it keeps a permanent record of attendance, grades, syllabi, and daily activities that happen in a classroom. These records give a picture of the pace at which students are progressing and the level and rigor of materials the teacher is using. Best yet, it keeps caregivers informed of their students' progress. Second, supplemental materials, including materials that ordinarily would be put on reserve in the library because of copyright or rarity, can be posted for students to access during or out of school hours. Third, if a teacher is absent, there doesn't need to be a disruption of learning because there are many options: substitute teachers can access the materials, teachers can teach remotely, and students can access materials on their own.

Teachers need to experiment with using the data they can collect using technology to assess student learning on a daily basis. Technology offers many ways in which teachers can quickly and easily check individual progress without having a mountain of grading every night: quizzes, tests, self-checks, or other advance organizers. With this information teachers can then better judge the pace and rigor of the materials and the need for remediation. Teachers also need to work with stakeholders and business managers on collecting data they can use as comparative data to weigh their students' progress against classes in the school, district, state, and nation.

PROFESSIONAL DEVELOPMENT

Technology plays a key role in increasing the amount of professional development that is available to teachers and staff. It provides many opportunities for them to come together electronically with other professionals and participate in organized workshops and discussion groups via closed-circuit interactive television, live chats over the Internet, or teleconferencing. Teachers can also choose to use podcasts and listen or watch workshops when they are ready—after their kids are in bed, on Saturday afternoon, or while grocery shopping. Blogs and educational news sources allow teachers to read articles and then make comments that the author or others can respond to. Teacher-practitioner and scholarly journals can be accessed from school, university, or public libraries at home, after school, or during planning periods.

Electronic media are not going to replace sending educators and staff to professional conferences and workshops where they can interact with peers from other parts of the United States or the world. Technology does make it possible for them to build on their new relationships after the conference is over. This networking is important in discovering potential funders, learning about special offers and new products from industry, and taking leadership roles in organizations, which adds to professional boasting for the school.

ELECTRONIC MATERIALS

There still is much to be accomplished to bring electronic curricula and software to the level where it shows a national, overall systemic improvement in student learning. The first step is that teachers, business managers, and schools must take charge and leverage their position as buyers. It should never be forgotten that education is a huge, powerful industry. The purchasing power of teachers can rule. Companies spend countless dollars to conduct research into what tempts teachers to buy. They will raise the bar if schools do. There are thousands of small companies that have the capability, desire for a share of the educational market, and talent to produce high-quality teaching materials with local applications at a competitive price. But before all of this can happen, the educational community has to define the gold standard for electronic curricula and its infrastructure. Educators have to lead and business managers have to organize them to do so.

Companies that produce and sell products need to develop materials that can target specific teaching challenges and address the types of teaching techniques that teachers must use to match the many different learning styles and preferences of students. These materials must be innovative products that employ the interactive qualities that technology provides. Novelty factors must be used to motivate and direct students, not distract. Comprehensive or curriculum programs should have a variety of choice of materials that teachers can use for different teaching styles. For example, a program on the Civil War should allow teachers to use video, audio, pictures, graphs, and interactives according to what they believe is appropriate for their students. A variety of choices should also be made available to students so that when they access materials they can go first to an activity that will engage and encourage them to continue learning. Navigation should be easy, quick, and logical to the user.

MANAGING THE INTERNET AS A RESOURCE

The Internet gives all that it originally promised and more. However, the same quality that makes the Internet a great resource also permits many inaccurate, not-so-exemplary sites to exist. Everyone has been frustrated by looking up a subject and finding thousands of references, about half of which are broken links. Others are amateurish teaching attempts that are riddled with hidden advertisements or that contain propaganda for some outlandish or even legitimate cause, but propaganda just the same. What teachers do need to do is work with library and technology staff to create or demand reliable browsers or management systems that do the job of filtering and categorizing materials. Business managers should mediate between librarians and teachers to blend information management skills into everyday teaching.

EVALUATION AND ASSESSMENT OF MATERIALS

As schools become more accountable for learning, business managers need to mediate between stakeholders and the school so that they can ask the right research questions. For example, the federal government gives money to be sure that there is a fair and equal opportunity for all students. Their benchmarks and goals seek to ensure that the money they give does what was promised. No child in any state is left behind. However, business managers have to worry about the unique qualities of their school. They cannot sit back and light up a cigar if the majority of students are not only well above the national average in reading scores. The feds may be happy, but the local school board still demands more because businesses always have to retain current employees and show new candidates that the community schools reflect a high standard of living, exemplary education for their children, and solid real-estate values.

Evaluation of electronic materials added to the other mix of successful practices will require more investigation about how the mixture of activities can be adapted to target D- and C-level students who have a specific learning challenge that prevents them from earning higher grades. The question that needs to be asked is, What works to keep students advancing their cognitive level of understanding of concepts, processes, and critical thinking while they work to bring their reading skills to level? For example, an immigrant or first-generation student from Iraq or Brazil may not be able to read and write well but is developmentally ready to understand the concept of DNA replication. Or a group of students may not have had exposure or encouragement to read at home and are behind level on reading but are nevertheless smart students.

SUMMARY

The important job for business managers in managing technology is to advance the American one-room schoolhouse model from one in which the teacher is solely responsible for student learning to a model of an industry of learning where the entire school is immediately involved and integrated. What is the difference? Because of technology, each person in the school can and needs to provide an aspect of learning and is responsible for a degree of accountability for student learning. Teachers need the tools to provide materials for diverse learners, to use statistical data to diagnose what techniques and materials to use, and to incorporate information management to educate students so that they have problem solving skills as well as a firm foundation of knowledge. Information management needs to become an intrinsic part of the curriculum. Knowledge needs to be woven with critical-thinking skills and strategies for finding valid information—a job for librarians. Front-office staff need to be the communications and public relations hub that establishes the identity of the school and opens doors to stakeholders.

To accomplish this, business managers need to govern technology and make long- and short-term plans that set the technology goals of all areas of the school in one direction that responds to the unique and evolving learning challenges each school faces. From there, management can make plans to direct the policies and procedures for everyday maintenance, purchasing, and organization. This is all part of technology being a commodity like the phone or turning on the lights. Schools have worked hard to get it to that stage. The next stage is to set the bar higher for the development of educational programs and stabilize the hardware and software infrastructure. Business managers will be the leaders who accomplish this.

Chapter Seventeen

And Then There Was Mosaic

My background in informal evaluation began while working at the Cincinnati Museum of Natural History in the late 1980s, when it moved from its Gilbert Avenue facilities into the remodeled railroad building, Union Terminal. This was the dot-com era for the museums. They couldn't be built big enough or fast enough. But alongside this catastrophic growth was a deep seriousness about research on the quality and quantity of learning. That was partly because of the fact that museums were accountable for learning far before the grim reality hit schools; investors insisted on knowing what was happening with their money, and, unlike schools, museums relied on grants, gifts, and donations to keep themselves afloat. They have to prove not only that they are good but that they are better than the museum or zoo down the street.

DeVere Brut, the director at the time, and Deputy Director of Exhibits Sandy Shipley had an opportunity that most businesses never have: a chance to redo the entire museum from the ground up. They were about to bet the bank but wanted to take a more secure route. They brought in Chandler Screven, a behavioral scientist whose research was in museum exhibits, as a consultant to educate and engage the staff on how to conduct the research. As they built the new exhibits, they were able to use the old museum as a laboratory to pilot test exhibit components and text. On opening day at Union Terminal, the staff already knew they had winning exhibits capable of pulling in the number of visitors and funders needed to keep the complex open. Two of the exhibits developed during that time, "The Cavern: A World without Light" and the ice age exhibit, "Clues Frozen in Time," have passed the best test of all, time, as they remain the favorites of visitors.

While I was working on GSLC (Genetic Science Learning Center), attracting and training teachers on technology and the novelty of genetic science clouded every evaluation issue. However, on reflection, it is not unusual that informal educational institutions with backgrounds in exhibits were the leaders for developing effective teaching Web sites. Biology: Exploring Life (EL) was being developed on the edge of the advancement of the early majority of teachers, so there was more time to watch how students were reacting and how they were navigating Web sites. It was clear that the characteristics of electronic instruction more resembled an exhibit than a textbook. The evaluation techniques that museums use are valuable resources for developing materials.

My technology background started thirteen years ago while I was working on a pioneering project to create an online science tool for teaching genetics in high school. Observations and contacts from this project provided an inside glimpse of the pace and process of bringing technology into schools. At this time, the United States was losing an educational war with Japan. They were whipping our students' butts in science and math, and Congress had given the National Science Foundation (NSF) the arduous task of changing that. NSF was in charge of the Internet and viewed it as a way to accomplish this task by using it as a venue for delivering science curriculum.

NSF's first strategy was to open free use of the Internet to universities, schools, and informal educational institutions like museums and zoos. The next was to channel millions of federal dollars to scientists who were on the cutting edge of research, partnering them with educators to build online resources that would bring scientists into the classroom virtually. All of this would educate the next generation of scientists and enlighten the next generation of voters. The timing was optimal. The Human Genome Project, which was mapping the genes in chromosomes, was in its third year and had made genetic science a hot teaching topic as well as cocktail-party conversation. It was the perfect project to show how and what the Internet could contribute to improve science education.

At that time, the University of Utah had received a five-year grant from the Howard Hughes Medical Institute to develop the Natural History of Genes (NHG), now called the Genetic Science Learning Center (GSLC). I served as the project manager. The project was a joint partnership among the school of medicine, the Eccles Institute of Human Genetics in the department of genetics, and the Utah Museum of Natural History. The project was to educate and update Utah teachers about genetic science and then provide them with hands-on activities that they could do with their students. The plan was to build the activities, put them in suitcases, and mail them out to the schools. However, the equipment and reagents for the experiments were expensive and fragile, making kit maintenance and transportation to and from the schools expensive.

For weeks, everyone at GSLC had been e-mailing back and forth ideas on how to economically deliver the kits to schools that are widely separated by vast deserts and rugged mountains. Mosaic had just appeared as a magic, but primitive by today's standards, way to display graphics. Finally, we realized that the way in which everyone was exchanging information would also be the best way to reach all the teachers. The Internet would host the written materials, and the labs would be designed to use kitchen items instead of expensive equipment, reagents, organisms, and supplies. Teachers could read the labs at home, gather up the materials as they rushed around in the morning to get ready for work, and head out to school.

But how could that idea be sold? By commandeering a computer and hiring a couple of students, we figured out how to plug it in. And then the tough part—we learned HTML, the language of the Internet, so we could put up a design and text. There were no user-friendly editors to correct spelling or applications to keep everything from wandering around. We went to Dorothy Dart, head of outreach and public relations at the Eccles Institute of Human Genetics, to get her okay to present our idea to the partners. It took a couple of tries to get her computer hooked up, but we did it and proudly showed it to her.

The look of absolute horror on her face was breathtaking. Dorothy was new to science and technology and was schooled in public speaking and public relations. What she saw was a public-relations nightmare. The dark maroon background and yellow letters on the home page took almost fifteen minutes to download. Every other word was misspelled. The design wandered. We told her to click to the new page to see the activities. As she clicked, her ready smile returned. She began to visualize the potential of what the Internet could do. She smiled and looked at us. This was good, but we had a lot of work to do to bring the Web site up to its current quality.

This was 1993, an exciting time for technology as well as for genetic science. The information superhighway or the World Wide Web, as it was intermittently called, was on its way to becoming a household word. Today, we just call it the Internet. It held the promise of doing what print media could not: instantly displaying new information with color graphics, movies, and animation that could be quickly updated and expanded. It would also be much cheaper than print media. Putting something on the Internet was free. It was the way for GSLC staff to update and deliver hot-out-of-the-labs curricula. This was a bold move, because using the Internet for education was a theory, not a practice.

There were some challenges. The Internet was so new that few teachers had access. Luckily for GSLC, Michael Leavitt, Utah's forward-thinking governor, was wiring schools at the speed of light. He was determined that every school in Utah would be connected to the Internet within the next couple of years. He was not only a man of vision but also someone who achieved his goals. GSLC calculated that if they worked fast, the lab directions and instructional materials would be up and running by the time the last school was online.

The next challenge was that the Internet was just a series of computers exchanging text documents and separate images; it was amazingly user-unfriendly. But in another stroke of innovation, Mosaic, the first browser, was invented. It made the Internet come alive by automatically retrieving files and arranging them in a mosaic of pictures and text. Even though computers had been around since the 1980s, for educators the Internet was really born when it became user-friendly and visually appealing. Until that time, the Internet had been a weird set of complicated protocols, text, and symbols. Mosaic was the catalyst that fired up the general public, and especially educators, to use the Internet.

So GSLC began, with Mosaic slowly downloading and unfolding information pages with the promise of eventual speed to match the breakneck pace with which the Human Genome Project was advancing genetics research, ethics, genetic counseling, conservation genetics, and health care. The goals were accomplished and expanded, just not according to the original plan; but nothing happens as per the original plan. A surprise audience was students who, excited about genetics, wanted to do the activities at home, for science fairs, or just for fun. Extracting DNA from fresh produce or meat in the refrigerator was a killer party activity.

It was a typical first-generation Web site: colorful backgrounds, white font, pictures, and lots of scrolling, with long lists of links to other resources. The original Web site incorporated a lot of color, graphics, and moving parts. Free visuals of karyotypes, gel runs, cells, scientists in the lab, and so on came from the research activities of the project partners. A fourteen-year-old boy genius, William Aoki, came in every day after high school and untangled the mess that the staff-turned-amateur-Web-designers had made of the site. The site was greatly enhanced when simple animation, like shuffling an image on the backs of cards, became possible. Primitive or not, the dancing and flashing was hot.

As GSLC was originally conceived, delivering kits to teachers over a period of five years, it only had a potential of reaching fifty or so science teachers during that time and, without additional funding, had no sustainability after the cash ran out. This was for many reasons. One was that genetics could only be taught at a certain time of the year; that meant all the teachers wanted kits at the same time. Another reason was that in order to use the electrophoresis equipment teachers had to have a high level of skill and training. Until more teachers were trained, only a handful could use the equipment. The third was that the time required for shipping and maintenance was greater than the time the kit would be at a school. Holidays greatly cut into the school year. No one wanted a kit right before or after a break. No one wanted a kit at the beginning of the year. No one wanted a kit at the end of the year. Only a handful of days were convenient.

Once GSLC switched to the Internet and kitchen chemistry, it greatly expanded its reach and success. The first users were a small but powerful group of teachers who, mostly at their own initiative, began to use computers. These were the early adopters, the unofficial and unheralded leaders of educational technology. They were inspired by adventure and raced ahead to find ways to use computers and other technology. They liked the idea of accessing lessons when they needed them and not waiting in line for their turn. They loved downloading the activities and spreading them around to other teachers.

GSLC was an excellent model for NSF's original plan of seeding and developing free Internet resources. It caught on quickly but still had to prove its effectiveness. This required intervention from the staff in ways that were not originally predicted. Staff had to train teachers to use the Internet, then sit back and watch how teachers would use it. To accomplish this, the staff had to go into the schools as well as offer workshops on campus. The newness of the lab activities and the Web site created a need to pilot test the lab protocols, navigation, and success with student learning. This kept the staff in constant, close, and personal contact with schools and professional organizations. But it didn't stop in Utah. Staff also went to national conferences.

Through all this, GSLC staff watched as schools advanced into the technology age and the Internet matured as a resource. The Web site reaching a broader audience and affecting more teachers than anticipated in the original project caused satisfaction, but it also brought another, scarier, realization. The Web site was going to be expensive to maintain. Therefore, GSLC kept in close contact with funders, both government and private. The project was a front-row seat to the holistic process of electronic delivery of curriculum. This has kept the site alive and vibrant.

The other Internet case study that is presented in this book began in 2000 with Biology: Exploring Life (EL).[1] EL is a high-school biology program that blends a traditional textbook, electronic learning activities, and hands-on lab exercises. Students read the textbook, do the related interactive activities on the computer, and then move to the lab to do the hands-on exercises. This program was unique because it was a complete curriculum that was used for an entire year. Before Exploring Life, textbooks only had supplemental activities haphazardly burned to CDs and stuffed in a jacket in the book's binding to be used if the teacher wanted. CDs were not an integral part of the program or teaching strategy.

Another unique aspect was that the publisher housed and maintained the electronic portion on a secure Web site to which the students logged in. This

---

1. I served as the on-site evaluator to help with the formative and summative evaluation. Dr. Al Bodzin of Lehigh University and Brad Williams, one of the coauthors, were the principal investigators. Dr. Ward Cates, Lehigh University, was the outside evaluator.

provided standardization and a guarantee of high-quality information because the publisher and authors could easily update and add to the program each year. Students and teachers had 24/7 access, which later proved to be one of the best aspects. Housing the site with the publisher guaranteed that the program could be accessed by any computer that was mildly modern and connected to the Internet. This also added value, because schools had motley computers of different brands, speeds, and memory.

EL was envisioned when a biology textbook author, Neil Campbell, noticed that high-school teachers were ordering his college introductory biology book to use for Advanced Placement (AP) courses in which students earned college credit in high school. Intrigued with what was going on in precollege science education, Neil began working with the AP teachers. They helped him to see that there was a real need for better teaching materials in the ninth-grade general biology courses. For many students, this would be the last science course they would take. He decided to create a general biology program that would provide multiple ways for students to learn by combining textbooks, computers, and labs.

To author and produce the program, he teamed up with Robin Heyden, an educational consultant, and Brad Williams, a high-school biology teacher. But like any textbook, they also needed artists, editors, and graphic designers. To add to that, unlike a regular textbook, EL required technical people and instructional designers to create the Web design, navigation, and interactive activities. This was an expensive proposition that required the type of big and long-term venture financing only a large publishing company could manage. Once EL was completed, it had to have a massive, national sales force that could quickly get it out to the market. Neil looked to his publisher, but, unlike his textbooks, which were proven sellers, EL was a hard sell.

Neil's proposal was untimely. He conceived of the project at the height of the dot-com boom, when it was easy to electrify people about anything remotely connected to technology. But in 2000, the fizzling dot-com frenzy caused venture capitalists to take a critical look at the bottom line. Where is the money? they asked. The first round of well-funded educational Web sites was fading fast, and the second round of funding was not coming through. The Internet was littered with abandoned Web sites that couldn't sustain themselves beyond the initial funding.

In 2000, the effectiveness of learning via electronic curriculum was not well understood, and the publisher still was not convinced that this type of program would sell. The publisher's reasoning was based on the fact that educational materials are sold largely on teacher recommendations. Tested, tried, and true was the greatest selling tool, and there was nothing tested, tried, or true about this program. The daily computer component added a certain edginess that made it provocative as the first product that relied on technology, but it was also risky. Not all teachers were comfortable with or sold on electronic media. In fact, there were teachers who prided themselves on not using technology.

What the publisher wanted was some type of positive sign from the education gods that would ensure the product could sell, or a warning so it could be dropped before too much money was spent on the development. EL needed some type of ongoing evaluation to show it would work and stimulate the teacher network. NSF came to the rescue, because they and their grant recipients had developed formative and summative procedures on how to evaluate educational programs as they were being developed.

In the education world, formative evaluation sounds unique, but it is not. It is commonly used in industry for product development. The process is very similar to how television programs are produced. The producers make one or two pilot episodes, which are shown to focus groups whose opinions ultimately determine if a network will consider financing a couple of episodes. After that, it is not over. Throughout the first season, focus groups and viewer surveys are conducted to determine program sustainability. Even after the program survives the first season, the formative evaluation continues as the program is aired. If viewers don't watch and focus groups report they don't like it, the program is yanked off the air. The formative evaluation guides the plot. The final or summative evaluation is based on whether it sells or not.

Formative evaluation can save money by preventing a failing product from being put onto the market, but it is still expensive—very expensive. Neil and his fellow authors approached NSF for funding. The EL evaluation was a good opportunity for NSF to have its evaluation techniques used by a large commercial publisher in the creation of an innovative project. It was also an excellent chance for them to get a snapshot of where educational technology was seven years after Mosaic and what would happen over the three years the project was developing. NSF agreed, and Neil, Robin, and Brad made three sample modules with a printed text, electronic activities, and labs. Then, over three years, one hundred teachers were involved in focus groups and/or pilot tests. Students were pre- and post-tested on their ability to learn basic concepts and surveyed about their attitude toward science and using computers to learn. Teachers were also surveyed about their success in administering the program and their attitude toward using computers. The reports were given to the development team to weigh as they created the program.

Soon after the evaluation started, it became quite apparent that the infrastructure was not where it originally had been expected. Therefore, the site visits began to include the principal, systems manager, and anyone else who was involved in providing technical support, training, management, or money. The evaluation proved that using computers, unlike other technologies, for learning is a group sport—it requires a team of experts. The haphazardness of each school's struggle to get computers to students sometimes overshadowed and controlled what was happening with the curriculum. This was not good. Over the three years, conditions began to change, and technology infrastructure began to mature; however, it became quite clear that the process of managing technology and the process of using it for teaching needed to be equally understood.

At the beginning of these projects, technology was a novelty. There was only excitement that it might work, no guarantees. Now, technology has advanced to become a commodity for schools. That is, it is somewhat like the telephone, gas for heating, and electricity. The path to this point was not easy and was, understandably but frustratingly, focused on machines and infrastructure. However, the slow adoption has also given educators time to build realistic models and plans for the next step, which is improving teaching and learning.

Another project that was influential in the writing this book is not a public school product but does employ the teaching strategies and opportunities that technology can provide. This one is still in development. AdjunctImpact was built in a partnership with Scott Taylor at bcpLearning while we did formative evaluation at the University of Texas at Brownsville. It is an electronic management system to aid college administrators in providing teaching support services to adjunct professors, a training program for adjuncts, and ongoing communication to continually connect everyone. Most students don't realize it, but adjunct professors teach as many as 50 percent of the classes they take. Adjuncts are usually professionals in the community who have another job and teach one or two classes a semester. The money is nice, but the pay is so little and the work so time-consuming it is hard to believe that they do it for any other reason than wanting to share with students. Adjuncts also appeared during the dot-com era. Technology is expensive, and colleges unabashedly began hiring adjuncts as a way to save money. The saved money did not enrich the coffers of colleges, but was used to absorb the rising cost of providing education in a technological world.

AdjunctImpact uses the 24/7 convenience of technology. Adjuncts are busy people and need to have answers and resources when they need them and when they can access them. The teaching strategy of AdjunctImpact is to provide them with the information they need only as they need it. It is pretty predictable. For example, when adjuncts get their first assignments, they are concentrated on the first day, mostly because they are usually hired within a week of when they will teach the class. They are focused on surviving the first day, so they see that information. As they progress, they discover they need to write tests. How do you write a test? That information is provided at 3 p.m. on Sunday or 10 p.m. on Thursday.

These are all people with advanced degrees, but they don't want to read the great American novel. They want easy and quick-to-read information. The information is layered, with each layer progressively delivering more complex information. If the information is not what they want, they can glance to the navigation menu, abandon where they are, and find where they want to be. The information is dotted with interactive activities that are entertaining and enjoyable but also informative. Even with adult learners, interactivity is important.

Each department hires adjuncts. The chair of the chemistry department hires the chemistry adjuncts, and the chair of the English department hires the English adjuncts. The administration ensures that adjuncts hired in each department have an opportunity to be connected with the college support services. Retention of students until they complete their degrees is a major issue in higher education. Since adjuncts are more likely to teach lower-level courses, it is important that they are prepared not only to teach but also to guide students to other career-building opportunities. For example, AdjunctImpact includes a list of student services, one of which is disability services, and a one-sentence explanation of how that service can help students who are bright but struggling in class.

All of these projects show the value of educational technology in solving local problems with local solutions. GSLC found a way to inform teachers about the basic principles of genetic science and the cutting-edge discoveries that are changing the way we do health care in the United States. Every year, the site grows more diverse to serve a greater number of people as more questions arise. Exploring Life gives teachers alternatives so they can just pick and choose. There is no hunting down Web sites or cutting and pasting of information to bring it to the level of students. Planning time is concentrated on teaching, not on hunting. AdjunctImpact solves the problem of roping in hard-to-corral users by ensuring that all adjuncts get the same high quality of support across campus.

About the Author

Betsy Price is an eclectic educational researcher who began her career developing programs for the Cincinnati Museum of Natural History and Science. After learning about the Internet and noticing the similarities to exhibit design she took the natural plunge into developing and evaluating educational programs on the Internet. As a volunteer producer/programmer she has produced and starred in Museum Notes and Talk for the Animals, programs for KRCL Community Radio in Salt Lake City.

She is currently an associate faculty member at The University of Texas at Brownsville working in adjunct faculty professional development. She heads the Support Office for Part Time Faculty and is Co-Developer of AdjunctImpact, a professional development portal for adjuncts.